The TOUCH of GRACE

The TOUCH of GRACE

ELIZABETH FULLER

Dodd, Mead & Company
New York

No part of this book may be reproduced in any form
without permission in writing from the publisher.
Published by Dodd, Mead & Company, Inc.
79 Madison Avenue, New York, N.Y. 10016
Distributed in Canada by
McClelland and Stewart Limited, Toronto
Manufactured in the United States of America

Designed by Judith Neuman
First Edition

1 2 3 4 5 6 7 8 9 10

Library of Congress Cataloging-in-Publication Data

Fuller, Elizabeth, 1946–
    The touch of grace.

    1. Amazing Grace (Evangelist)   2. Healers—United
States—Biography.   3. Evangelists—United States—
Biography.   4. Spiritual healing.   I. Title.
BT732.56.A43F85   1986   234′.13   85-27373
ISBN 0-396-08667-5

For Cary and Maryann

PREFACE

WHEN I COMPLETED THIS BOOK AND REREAD it, I have to confess that I had mixed feelings. The strange and powerful events that unfolded over the entire year I spent with Grace were as baffling as they were incredible.

Here was a radiant and vivid personality, responsible for thoroughly documented medical cures that could be described in no other way than as miraculous. To capture this on paper has been extremely difficult. As the cliché goes, "You had to be there." But thousands and thousands of people *have* been there, have witnessed the proceedings, and have been forced to acknowledge that what Grace accomplishes is genuine.

However, as a nontheological type, I had trouble accepting the way in which Grace accomplishes her work. How can a simple touch on someone's forehead cause that person to topple over and get up again almost instantaneously, free of disabilities? This was the question I constantly put to Grace. And just as constantly, she would answer that it was the power of Jesus Christ, who was working through her.

I reminded Grace that such an explanation—as true as it may be—would not go over with the general public. We live in a scientific age, when miracles rank somewhere below Donald Duck on the scale of believability. Grace's response to that was simple and to the point: "Liz, you're free to explore all possible avenues. But I'm telling you, when you're done, you'll see that what I'm saying is true."

In an effort to satisfy everyone, I set out over this last year not to negate what Grace was saying but to try to find some sort of rational explanation, one that would be palatable to those of us who need more than blind faith to believe in miracles. Simply, I was trying to strike a balance between religion and science, between reason and faith.

Grace more than willingly went along with this plan. Her records of those who have been healed through the ministry were opened to me. The names of doctors and their patients were also given to me, along with four years of video and audio tapes of the services. Furthermore, I was given carte blanche at all services to interview those who claimed to have had healings and to follow up on their cases. At no point did there appear to be anything the least bit clandestine going on. I observed no shills at the services or pretending on the part of those testifying to their healings. Grace encouraged me to bring members of the medical profession to the services; over the course of the year, I brought a dozen doctors who were impressed, even stunned, by what they saw, regardless of whether they accepted it in Grace's terms.

All the material and dialogue in the book has been carefully reconstructed from over forty hours of taped interviews that I conducted. From these interviews, certain facts became evident: Many people were suddenly and inexplicably healed. Medical specialists confirmed this. Although the diseases of some of the afflicted were too far along for any healing to take place, I did personally observe the very real sense of peace and comfort that came over several of these terminally ill people, along with a sharp reduction of pain and anxiety. Where there is no physical healing, Grace believes that there is a spiritual one. And there was plenty of evidence that people hopelessly addicted to drugs or alcohol were immediately able to terminate their addiction without any sign of withdrawal symptoms.

The result of my year's research, which included attending over fifty services, is that I have come no closer to a real explanation than when I first started out. Perhaps my reaction is best summed up by a quotation from NASA scientist Robert Jastrow, who wrote at the end of his book *God and the Astronomers*, "For the scientist who has lived by his faith in the power of reason, the story ends like a bad dream. He has scaled the mountains of ignorance; he is about to conquer the highest peak; as he pulls himself over the final rock, he is greeted by a band of theologians who have been sitting there for centuries."

The TOUCH of GRACE

CHAPTER ONE ❧❧

THE SERVICE TAKING PLACE IN THE CAVERNOUS Catholic church called St. Thomas Aquinas in New York City was far from the conventional Catholic mass. The congregation was mixed. There were black families, Hispanic families, white families. There were Protestants, Catholics, and Jews—well over a thousand people were jammed into the pews and packed along the walls.

On a raised platform in front of the altar was a striking figure in a long flowing gown, with jet-black hair and dark, flashing eyes. She was singing a song called "God of Miracles" with such power and persuasion that the audience sat in stunned silence. When she was finished, thunderous applause reverberated against the vaulted ceiling.

As the applause died down, a woman known as Amazing Grace walked down the center aisle, microphone in hand, silent, her eyes scanning the rows of people. One by one, she pointed to specific persons, naming their infirmities, asking each to move forward to the base of the altar. Some hesitated; others rose quickly and walked down the aisle; some hobbled on crutches. Others came forward in wheelchairs.

There were roughly thirty in the group by the time Grace rejoined them in front of the altar. "You will see many healing miracles here this afternoon," Grace said. "But I want you to know that it is not I who is doing the healing. It is Jesus."

Her message was simple and direct. Open your hearts to God, and He will do the healing. Anything is possible through the Lord.

"And remember," Grace added. "I'm not here to replace your own congregation of whatever denomination. Nor am I here to replace your doctors. God works with all of us in many ways."

She moved across the line of people now facing her at the front of the church. As she did, each confirmed the ailment she had designated. She moved swiftly, touching them lightly on their foreheads. Nearly three out of four fell over backward into the arms of the ushers, who eased them gently down to the floor. Some remained there for as long as five or ten minutes. Others sat up, dazed. Some remained standing.

"Many of you have just experienced what is called falling out in the Spirit. Some of you have merely been touched. Either way, you are feeling the healing power of Jesus as He continues to minister to us, healing the sick, working miracles."

A five-year-old child lay stunned on the floor, her Cabbage Patch doll resting in her arms. A crippled nun rose from the floor without help, and as Grace took her metal walker away, she asked her to walk to her. The nun did—the first time she had walked in five years, she said. Grace told her to run up the aisle. She did—

and the audience applauded. A deaf man responded to a whisper from Grace and then claimed that he was hearing for the first time in over a decade. An elderly woman claimed she had been scarcely able to leave her home for three decades. When Grace prayed over her, she finally got up the courage to face the audience and said, "I felt the warmth in my body. I knew that God was healing me. I felt peace and calm come over me." A woman who had suffered for nearly a year from a slipped cervical disc, taking pain-killers every four hours and lying in traction three days a week, removed her cervical collar and claimed an instant cure.

The procession continued, with scores of people coming forward. Many claimed full relief from their afflictions. At the end of the service, a priest stood up in the audience and declared loudly, "I have seen Christ come alive here tonight."

As a journalist, I watched the scene, incredulous. My first impulse was to dismiss it as a fantasy. I was puzzled, curious, disbelieving. All through the evening, I kept saying to myself, This can't be true. There must be some sort of rational explanation for what is happening. But the more I tried to figure out what that was, the more baffled I became. I left thinking that either it was the most incredible thing since Jesus at Gallilee or it was a great carnival show.

For days afterward I was haunted by the memory of what I had seen. Cautiously, I told a few of my more open-minded friends. But even they didn't buy it. Some merely discounted the whole experience as mass hysteria. Others claimed she must use hypnosis to get the people to fall over. And still others said that all those people dropping crutches and getting out of wheelchairs were obviously shills. Although my friends may have had a point about mass hysteria and hypnosis, I felt that the shill theory was weak, simply because Grace would have had to hire busloads of them and own a fleet of wheelchairs, besides. But I was in no position to argue on Grace's behalf. For all I knew, my friends were right.

However, I was determined to go again and take my husband along for his opinion. John is an investigative journalist who has written books exposing everyone and everything from the stock market to the Food and Drug Administration. I was hopeful that he would be able to shed some light on what was happening. In addition, he had been troubled for over a year with arrhythmia—an irregular heartbeat—that simply would not respond to medicine. Perhaps he would be a test case, more or less, although I didn't tell him that.

Two weeks later, John and I were sitting in the back of a crowded high school auditorium in Greenwich, Connecticut, watching a complete rerun of what I had seen that first time. There were people leaving their wheelchairs, deaf ears were opening, cataracts and glaucoma were disappearing, depression was lifting, and alcoholics were being delivered. Again, I found it impossible to believe that these people were actually being healed.

I couldn't tell what John was thinking. He was sitting stone silent. Occasionally he would shrug his shoulders, as if to indicate bewilderment. But he didn't appear to be bored. He kept his eyes planted on Grace, watching as she glided effortlessly up and down the aisles in a pale pink chiffon gown. One by one, Grace continued to call out various types of illnesses and asked for the persons to come forward and claim their healings.

4

How did Grace know the section where the people who needed healings were seated? I got up the courage to ask the rather tweedy and well-groomed man next to me. I figured he might know because after each person was healed he shouted, "Thank you, Jesus!" And then he would clap as if Joe DiMaggio had slammed one out of the park. The man simply answered me that it was the "word of knowledge." I nodded as if that all made perfect sense.

However, I became suspicious of this word of knowledge when Grace stood between two rows, stretched out her right arm toward those sitting there, moved her slender fingers as if they were antennae, and said that there was someone sitting nearby with cancer. When no one stood up to claim the healing, I thought that Grace might have just been lucky half the night, safely calling out common illnesses. But then Grace pointed to a man about five feet from her and told him that it was he she was talking about, and would he please stand. The man hesitated before he got up. He didn't look sick to me. I was waiting for him to tell Grace that it was a mistake, that he was the wrong person. But Grace didn't give him a chance. She promptly began to diagnose his condition. "Sir, you have throat cancer," she said, looking him straight in the eyes.

From where I was sitting, several rows back, it looked as if she could see right through him, almost as if she had some sort of X-ray vision.

"You've had it for several months. And you've been in severe pain for the last two weeks," she went on. "I want you to come forward for your healing."

Then she turned on her heels and headed for the center of the auditorium, exuding such self-confidence that I was actually worried for her. I was convinced

5

that she was about to embarrass herself and the man following her. In fact, the man didn't appear all that anxious to go for a healing. But the person next to him, who must have been his wife, gave him a slight nudge to get moving.

Once they reached the center of the auditorium, Grace made an invisible cross on his forehead with her thumb. Her head was tilted slightly back. Her eyes were turned heavenward. Then she said with firm authority, "Be healed in the name of Jesus!"

Immediately, the man fell backward into an usher's waiting arms. He lay on the floor as if he had been knocked unconscious. A full five minutes later, he got to his feet, straightened out his sweater vest, and shook his head as if to give himself a reality test.

Grace was as confident about his healing as she had been about his diagnosis. "Jesus just healed you," she said. "How do you feel?"

The man, still dazed, wrapped his hand around his throat and began to swallow. Suddenly a tentative smile came over him as he said that it was the first time in weeks that he had no soreness from the throat cancer.

With that, the audience began clapping. Some began praising Jesus. Guitar music filled the auditorium. Grace flung her arms high in the air, shouted "Hallelujah," and then broke out into a fast-tempo song her guitarist had written called "I've Got the Faith." The man sitting next to me was clapping so enthusiastically that I almost wished I had his faith.

His enthusiasm *was* catching, however. As Grace lifted her voice in a fresh new rhythm, I clapped and mouthed the repetitious lyrics along with all the others. I felt like a holy roller, but I had good company— John was doing the same thing. However, when he noticed me looking at him, he casually folded his arms and took on one of his superior, journalist's looks.

One thing was certain: Grace had the ability to captivate and hold the attention of hundreds of people.

Two hours into what would be a four-hour service, Grace asked all those who had been healed through the ministry to please raise their hands. About fifty hands went up, including that of the man sitting next to me. Grace then asked for some of them to give a quick testimony of their healing. The first to stand was a young couple who said that they had been addicted to drugs and had been in and out of various drug rehabilitation centers for five years, but nothing had worked. It wasn't until they came to a service and received a healing that they were cured, with no withdrawal symptoms.

The next to stand was an elderly Catholic nun. She said that she had had Paget's disease—a progressive degenerative disease that softens the bones—and had been confined to a wheelchair for over ten years. But after being touched by Jesus through Grace three years ago, she said, she'd been walking ever since. To prove the point, Grace asked that she take a walk around the auditorium. As the cherubic-looking nun moved from her seat, the guitarist, who managed to create the illusion of a full band, segued into a joyous bluegrass gospel song called "He Set Me Free." Once again, the audience began clapping. The nun clapped too, keeping in time with the beat, almost dancing down the aisle.

The moment the music died down, a woman in her fifties stood and said that during a service six months before, her depression had left, never to return. Grace's answer to that was a soft, drawn-out "Praise Jesus!" Next, Grace called on a pretty blond girl sitting in a wheelchair. "Honey," Grace said, "what did God do for you?"

The girl, with all the enthusiasm of a high school cheerleader, called back, "He made me happy again!"

One of the last to give a testimony was the man sitting next to me, but instead of speaking from his seat as the others had, Grace asked him to come forward. Before he did, his wife passed him a large manila envelope, which he tucked underneath his arm. Then he jogged down the aisle and up to the stage platform, leaping up two steps at once, wasting no time.

Unlike the rest of the people who testified to healings, this man appeared to be as conscientious about the details of his healing as he was about his perfectly tailored wardrobe. He said that his name was Anthony DeBernardi. He was sixty-nine years old. And he was a recently retired advertising manager from a division of Gulf + Western.

"Twenty-six months ago, I went to see my doctor," he began. "I didn't feel well. And he sent me to a radiologist. It was there that I got the bad news: He said that I had lung cancer. But I didn't really believe it. Although I was sick, I didn't feel that bad. So I went for a second opinion. I was told the same thing. But I still went for a third opinion, this time to Sloan-Kettering in New York. The verdict was carcinoma of the left lung. I went back to my internist, and he said, 'Tony, it hurts for me to tell you this. But you have to go into the hospital right away. You can't wait any longer.' I followed his advice and made an appointment for the next week.

"But three days later, I became very sick. I began to hurt so that I could barely breathe. The pain got worse. I couldn't stand. I couldn't sit. I could hardly lie down,"

8

he said. "I began to run high temperatures—101, 102, 103, 104. I frankly wished that I didn't have to breathe anymore. I was that sick.

"While the temperature was 104, my wife dialed Grace's prayer line. We had been to one of her services three years earlier on my sister's suggestion. And we were astonished at what we had seen." He stopped to smile and nod toward Grace, who was at his side holding the microphone.

"It was just a little past midnight when the phone rang," he continued. "It was Grace. She said, 'Would you like me to pray for you?' I said yes. And while she prayed, I began to get very warm. Hot. I began to perspire. Grace told me that I was not going to feel well for a couple of days, but that after that, I was going to be completely healed. Although I didn't realize it at the time, I think the healing was instantaneous. I went to bed that night and slept like a baby.

"In the morning, the pain had disappeared. I started to feel great. I felt so good that I began to eat. But a few days later it was time to go into the hospital." He paused a moment, smiled, and added, "When they took more X-rays, the radiologist discovered that the tumor was no longer there. The doctors immediately began to compare the before-and-after X-rays and CAT scan. The only thing left on the new set of X-rays was a tiny scar where the tumor had been."

At that point, his voice softened to the point that it almost sounded as if he were choking back tears. However, he quickly regained his composure and continued. "The following day, I was sent home from the hospital with a clean bill of health. My doctor said, 'Tony, I can give you a certificate to join the marines!' "

Then, just before he left the stage area, he held up

9

the large manila envelope. It contained his before-and-after X-rays as visual proof, if anyone was interested. The last thing he said was, "Thank you, Jesus!"

I was embarrassed to feel tears welling up in my eyes. I thought, no wonder he was so enthusiastically clapping each time someone claimed to have been healed. If that had happened to me, I probably would have reacted in the same way.

But the tears were short-lived. My suspicions took over again. I wondered what the alternative medical explanation was. I would have liked to see a couple of doctors step out of the audience and take a look at his X-rays. But I doubted that doctors went to see healers performing "miracles."

When the man came back to his seat, I turned to him and said that I was very moved by his healing. He thanked me and then introduced his wife, Nina. As we shook hands, both said almost at the same time that God had been good to them. Their sincerity was genuine.

"I want the man right over there to come up," Grace was saying. She pointed to the back of the auditorium and added, "The little guy."

The "little guy" turned out to be a strapping, 250-pound, jolly-faced Italian called Foey. He ran up onto the stage, tenderly placed an arm on Grace's shoulder, and told what had happened to him nine months earlier.

"That first night my wife dragged me here," he began, "I made her sit way back in the last row. I had very bad back pain from a slipped disc. I was in so much pain that I was taking twelve codeine pills a day. I was crawling around my house like an animal. No one knows back pain until they've had it. I had gone to different doctors, chiropractors. I had needles, electric vibrators six days a week. Nothing worked. That night I came to a service with a cane. It took me twenty minutes to walk from the car to my seat.

"When the first few people you prayed for fell over, I didn't believe it," he said to Grace. "I said to myself, 'Foey, you crazy for coming to something like this?' I told my wife that if Grace touches me and I fall over, then it's for real, because I was so hunched over, the only way I could fall would be forward. But then there was this deaf girl sitting in front of us. She was eighteen years old. After you prayed for her, she could suddenly hear. She began crying. The whole family was crying, even her father. And I saw that happen. And I said, 'Well, Foey, maybe something is goin' on.' So all of a sudden I began praying that she'd call on me. Next thing I knew, Grace called on me. I looked around, thinking that it couldn't really be me. But my wife said that it was me. I went up, and the next thing I knew I was on the floor. On my back. I didn't even know how I got there. I got up with no cane, no nothing. The pain was gone. I began to cry like a baby." Then he added with sudden reverence, "Thank you, Jesus."

"Did you ever think that you'd be saying 'Thank you, Jesus' in front of five hundred people?" Grace asked.

"Never could happen. Now, when I go to my club and I tell the boys what Jesus did for me, they all say, 'There he goes again. Old Foey's gone religious on us.' "

John and I chuckled over Foey's story. But suddenly Grace had swept up the aisle and clasped her hand around John's wrist. Within seconds they were headed down the aisle, Grace in her flowing white gown, delicately trimmed in lace, John in his wrinkled Harris tweed jacket that should have been pitched during the

Eisenhower administration, and khaki slacks with a pipe hanging over the edge of the side pocket.

When they reached the apron of the stage, Grace let go of John's hand. An usher moved forward and placed him at the end of the healing line, where he became number seven. Then Grace stopped singing and announced that while she prayed for each person, we should pray too.

Grace stood before the first person in the line. He was a thick-set man of about fifty, with a full head of hair. When she placed her two fingers on his forehead, he wavered, looking a little bit like Bozo-the-tipping-clown. Grace wrapped her arms around his shoulders to steady him. Then she moved behind him and began to run her hand along his spine; he had a slipped disc. Her eyes were closed, and she had begun to speak in what sounded like a foreign language, Spanish, I thought. But it wasn't a language at all, at least not an earthly one. I later learned it was called "Glossalalia," or speaking in tongues, a phenomenon referred to throughout the Bible. According to Grace, "As you're praising and thanking God, you may get to the point where your tongue just doesn't seem to be able to speak English anymore. That's the Holy Spirit coming forth, speaking a heavenly language that only God understands."

After several minutes, Grace opened her eyes. No longer speaking in tongues, she asked the man how his back felt. He tentatively pulled his shoulders back and did some sort of stretching motion. Then he announced loudly and clearly that the pain from his slipped disc was gone. Grace wasn't satisfied with just that. She asked him to touch his toes. Without a second's hesitation, the man reached down and touched his toes, not once but three times. It was the first time since the army that he could remember doing that, he said. And in the last few years, he added, the pain had become so severe that his wife had to help him get his socks on.

Just before he returned to his seat, Grace asked if he had come expecting a miracle. The man gave a rather sheepish grin toward the audience, lowered his head, and admitted that he hadn't. But he quickly added that his wife had. He said that his wife and daughter had brought him there in the hope that something like this would happen.

"Well, hallelujah!" Grace shouted, throwing one arm up in the air and the other around his plump middle. "You believe now?" she asked with total confidence.

"You betcha," he said. "And believe me, I never thought anything like that could ever happen to me."

"Praise God! Our God is a God of miracles. He's alive. And He's here tonight. This is just the beginning! Just keep praising and thanking God for the miracle in your life," Grace said, as the man ran up the aisle like a tight end for the Pittsburgh Steelers.

The next person in the line was also a middle-aged man; he was wearing plaid slacks and a canary-yellow Arnold Palmer sweater. Grace dunked her two fingers into a crystal jar of anointing oil brought to her by an attractive young female usher. The moment she placed her fingers to his sun-tanned forehead, his knees buckled, sending him to the floor. He lay there with his eyes shut and lids quivering as if he were in the REM—rapid eye movement—stage of sleep. Grace didn't wait for him to get up. She casually stepped over the long plaid legs and moved on to the next person.

I watched John eyeing all these "miracles" happening before him. His body seemed to stiffen as Grace

13

inched her way nearer to him. She had reached the petite gray-haired woman in a slim camel-colored skirt and white sweater trimmed with tiny beads who was next to him. Grace tossed her raven-black head back and her eyes up, as if she were listening for divine instructions.

Seconds later, she backed up about a foot from the woman. Then, waving her entire arm in an up-and-down motion, in the manner of a symphony conductor cueing an allegro, she forcefully commanded, "Depression be lifted in the name of Jesus!" With that, the woman collapsed backward into an usher's arms. She was out cold.

John was next. He had now strategically planted his L. L. Bean moccasins two feet apart, probably counting on some sort of celestial Krazy Glue to keep him standing. John had commented several times that he could never fall over, because it just wasn't part of his belief system. He also hated to fall backward. Now he didn't seem to be taking any chances.

When it came to religion, John and I felt very much the same way. We believed that all religions contained jewels of wisdom; it was just a matter of mining the jewels. We certainly didn't doubt that Jesus had been a wonderful prophet who had changed the course of history for the Western world more than anyone and that He must have been divinely sparked. The recent findings about the Shroud of Turin added scientific validity to that. But John and I also felt that Christianity was one of the many paths you could take up the mountain. Two of my favorite proverbs, which sum up how I felt, are, *No one religion has a corner on God; He owns the whole block,* and, *God has been cast in so many religions, it's amazing He always shows up knowing his lines.*

Grace looked as if she were about to lay hands on John, but then she turned and signaled for the female usher to bring the anointing oil to her. She submerged her two fingers into the crystal jar. Then she lifted them to John's forehead.

In retrospect, I never anticipated that John would join the man with the plaid slacks on the floor. If anything, I thought he might waver a little, perhaps even stumble around before regaining his footing. But I never thought I would see my six-foot, 175-pound husband go down like a bowling pin when five-foot-four, 115-pound Grace touched his forehead.

At the time when John was lying on the floor, unconscious, for several minutes, neither of us knew that his arrhythmia had been cured. It would take many months before he would be certain of that. At the service, when he got up and returned to his seat, all he knew was that the skipped heartbeats had suddenly stopped, to his amazement, to my amazement, and later to the amazement of his own doctor, who believed in miracles with the same intensity as he believed in the Tooth Fairy.

Once we left the auditorium and hit the soft August air, John no longer remained silent. "You know something?" he said, "I really don't know what to think. I've never seen anything like it. And that includes Africa, Brazil, Nepal—you name it."

"You believe what happened?"

"Well, I have to believe what happened to me. One minute I'm standing. The next I'm picking myself up off the floor."

"You think you're healed?"

"All I know is that the skipped heartbeats are not there," John said. "I hope it's not just temporary."

Driving along the Merritt Parkway toward home,

John began to wonder out loud about hypnosis, suggestion, mass hysteria, and other phenomena.

"She didn't try any sort of obvious induction, like the you're-getting-sleepier-and-sleepier type of thing," he said. "And she didn't particularly stare them in the eyes, either. I don't have the faintest idea how I fell over. She just seemed to point at me."

John was quick to add that, although Grace didn't use the type of hypnosis that he was familiar with, she did use suggestion. And that is the basis of hypnosis. Her suggestion was simply that Jesus would heal. That could account for why so many of those who fell backward were able to get up claiming that their pain was gone. They really believed that they had been healed. And Grace really believed that Jesus had healed. She appeared to have the very deepest kind of faith possible.

"For instance," John said, "you might say that because the nun had a deep religious faith, she was highly suggestible to the fact that Jesus was going to heal her. And *that* could be one reason why she was able to leave her wheelchair."

John seemed to be luxuriating in his newly formed hypnosis theory. This was not typical of him. In the past, he would never come to any definitive explanation without carefully weighing and examining all the evidence. But now, for some reason, he suddenly seemed comfortable explaining the whole thing away with a rational theory.

With an overconfident drag on his pipe, he went on. "Another reason she was able to leave her wheelchair could be adrenaline. It's sometimes brought on in a stressful situation. People might do things they could never do under normal conditions."

"But the rush of adrenaline is only a temporary con-

16

dition," I said. "It doesn't account for how that nun has been able to stay out of the wheelchair for the last three years. Or how her progressive bone disease went into spontaneous remission after being touched by Grace."

John thought about that for several moments before he said, almost reluctantly, "You're right. It's probably not just faith, or a rush of adrenaline, or hypnosis. There's something else going on."

CHAPTER TWO ❧❧

PERHAPS JOHN WAS RIGHT. MAYBE THERE WAS something else going on. It certainly looked that way during the service. And if—just if—all that Grace said was true, maybe she could help my close friend Cary in the tragic situation she was going through. At thirty-six, Cary was facing incurable cancer.

Along with the very dramatic physical healings, we had also seen dozens of people claim to have received inner healings—inner peace. With Cary's cancer so far advanced, it was this kind of healing that I hoped she could receive. At one point during the service John and I had attended Grace had asked all those who felt as if something were missing in their lives to come forward and accept Jesus as their personal savior. With soft guitar music playing, Grace spoke to the audience as if she were speaking to each person individually. That seemed to be part of her charisma.

"If you need a change in your life, try God. You won't regret it," Grace had said. "Maybe you're having financial problems? Problems with your children? Maybe you're depressed. You can live with being crippled, blind, or deaf, but you can't live with depression. Maybe you're addicted to drugs? Alcohol? Anything that is wrong in your life," she went on, "God will cure. You may have all the riches here on earth. But are you *truly* happy? Is there a void in your life? If you feel as if I'm speaking about you, then come on down and invite God into your hearts. Even if you don't believe there is a God," she added, "come forward and find out for yourself."

At the time, it all sounded too simplistic for my taste. But recalling the sight of a hundred or so people clustered in front of Grace, I suddenly had confidence that she could help Cary. I fell asleep that night wondering if Cary would be receptive to something like this. She was so strong-willed that she rarely even acknowledged the disease. At times, it seemed as if she wanted to fight her battle alone. If I did mention the idea to her, I would have to be careful not to give her false hope. Knowing Cary's down-to-earth sensibility, no hope at all would be better than false hope.

To eliminate any risk of that happening, I would avoid telling her about the people I had seen who claimed they had been cured of cancer. I would, however, mention the nun, since Cary was Catholic. I would of course also tell her about the feelings of inner peace many had spoken of. But before I said anything, I would first have to gently feel her out on the whole subject. And then if she were willing to go along with it, I would have to figure some way to get Grace to see her in the hospital. This would be a formidable job; Grace knew neither of us personally, and she had thousands clamoring for her attention.

The following morning, John and I talked at some length about how I should go about actually describing

Grace to Cary. John said what I already knew: Keep it low-key. Don't get into all the purported cancer healings, or all the people who dropped crutches and got out of wheelchairs. Offer no false hope.

Fortunately, I had picked up one of Grace's monthly magazines at the service and was able to find her twenty-four-hour prayer-line number. While dialing, I noticed a photo of a man I recognized as one of Grace's ushers. The headline read, NO MORE ALCOHOL! Below it was a quote that said, "I'm free. Believe me, I'm free!" I skimmed the article. It was certainly dramatic. He had been delivered not only from alcoholism in one brief instant, but also from a five-pack-a-day cigarette habit, plus a slipped disc. This seemed to be almost too much to believe.

My doubts began to surface once again. I was tempted to hang up the phone, when a voice came on the other end of the line.

"Prayer line," a young woman said. "May I help you?"

I explained that I was actually trying to get in touch with Grace personally, and did she know how I could do that? She said that she would take my message, name, and number and see that Grace got it. But she couldn't assure me when Grace would return the call, or even if she would return it at all.

An hour later, the phone rang. It was Grace. I immediately thanked her for returning my call, saying that I realized she probably got hundreds of calls. She did get a lot, she said, but her volunteers were very good and could handle most, usually by praying with the caller. However, the real emergencies she took care of herself. I suddenly hoped that she would consider my call a real emergency.

Grace didn't appear to be rushed. Instead of asking right away why I had phoned, she first wanted to know if I had ever been to a service. I said that I had been to two, and I told her which two. And I told her that I found them fascinating. But after I said "fascinating," I wished that I hadn't used that word. Suddenly I had a strange feeling that she knew I was not a real believer. But even if she did sense that, she didn't make me feel uncomfortable. At no time did she even try to convince me of anything. Instead, she said that she understood my skepticism. I was waiting for her to start quoting Scripture. But she never did.

When Grace learned that I was Catholic, she said that about seventy-five percent of those who come to her services are Catholic. A growing number of them are of the Vatican II Charismatic Christian Renewal group, sanctioned by Pope John XXIII in the early sixties. Grace said that she often worked side-by-side with bishops, monsignors, and priests. In fact, she said that recently a bishop from New York had come anonymously to a service and had received a healing. After that, he invited her to minister at his parish.

I'm not exactly sure how much longer we chatted before Grace finally asked about my friend with cancer. When she said "cancer," I was taken by surprise. I clearly remembered not having mentioned to her or to the prayer-line volunteer that Cary had cancer. I had simply said that she was very ill. I guess I felt the same way Cary did: Acknowledging the cancer was an admission of defeat.

How had she known that my friend had cancer? I asked. The word of knowledge, she replied. I wondered if this word of knowledge also told Grace how urgent I felt it was for her to visit Cary. Grace spared me the agony of having to ask that question; she offered to go to the hospital on Wednesday of the coming week. She said that she would stop by on the way to her Greenwich office, where she has private counselings each week.

It was all so strange. Neither Cary nor I was of a religious leaning, yet I was determined to have Grace see Cary, desperately hoping for a miracle. When I told Cary about Grace, she didn't verbalize any such hope. She didn't have to. Little things she said crept into the conversation. In fact, only minutes before Grace had returned my call, Cary had phoned, wanting to know if Grace was going to be able to come and see her. I told Cary that I was certain that Grace would.

I also told her about an article I had read that seemed to explain what might be happening at Grace's services. It concerned a lecture by well-known cancer specialist Dr. Carl O. Simonton. He stated, "As far as my belief-system goes—I know patients get well without any form of treatment. But as far as malignancy goes, we have people that are opened and closed and told to go home and die. From a medical standpoint there is no way that the person would get well whatever is done for them. But they do get well."

He added, "Something happens, and when analyzed, the small numbers that have been looked at, there seems to be a very possible, psychological socio-religious thing happening."

I wondered if Grace could trigger some "psychological socio-religious" thing to happen for Cary. The way her disease had been progressing, a miracle might be her only hope. And if a miracle didn't happen, there was still the comforting thought that Grace might be able to tacitly offer Cary peace of mind, something none of her friends or family had seemed to be able to do. Whatever happened, I suddenly felt that Grace would somehow be instrumental in Cary's life—or even in her untimely death.

The following day, I met Grace in the hospital lobby. Although I had never met her personally, we hugged hello. I had tears in my eyes.

"Don't worry, Liz," Grace said softly. "Cary's going to be just fine."

"Fine, alive?" I asked, thinking that maybe the word of knowledge had told her something before she even met Cary.

Grace didn't answer directly. Instead, she wanted to know if I had any children. I said I had one little boy, two years old. Why? I asked. She said that when she prayed over Cary, I should pray too. And that I should pray that God would take care of Cary with the same childlike trust my little boy has that I'll take care of him.

I told Grace that I would do that. But as we got off the elevator and headed down the long antiseptic corridor leading to Cary's room, I wished that Grace had said that of course Cary would be just fine. Fine, alive, that is.

Once in Cary's room, there was no exchange of small talk. That somehow didn't seem to be necessary. In fact, it appeared that Grace triggered the release of a vulnerability hidden within Cary, allowing her to express the pain locked inside.

"It's getting tougher and tougher," Cary said in answer to Grace's question of how she was feeling.

When Cary spoke those words, the pain throughout her body seemed to surface into her large expressive eyes. As Cary went on to describe her condition, I thought of all the energy it must have taken for her to mask her suffering from her family and friends. There was an incredibly private part of Cary that no one had been able to penetrate—at least not until now.

"I think I can accept death," Cary said, "but I'm

afraid that my husband, my family, and my friends can't."

"Let's pray," Grace said. "We're going to ask God to take this cancer from you."

She placed her hand over Cary's forehead and began. "Dear God, please lift this cancer—this pain—from Cary's body." Her eyes were closed, her head tilted upward. "In Jesus's name, give her peace, joy, and your healing love."

As Grace continued softly praying over Cary, I tried to do exactly what Grace had told me to do, pray with childlike trust that God would take care of Cary. But I couldn't. I was waiting for something miraculous to happen.

In one sense, nothing miraculous happened. In another sense, it did. Cary told us that she had felt a warm surge of energy pass through her entire body when Grace touched her forehead. It brought with it a kind of peace that she had never known before, a feeling of instant comfort and protection.

"Whatever happens," Cary said just before we left, "I know that it's right. And I accept."

She did accept. She died peacefully several weeks later. Before she died, she told me again about the warm surge that had gone through her when Grace had placed her hands on her forehead. She said that it was as if all the energy she had put into fighting the cancer had suddenly been transferred into the hands of God, that now He was dealing with the cancer. She felt as if she were now floating in a warm bath of sunshine instead of being trapped in a black thundercloud.

It moved me profoundly that Grace, with her busy schedule, had responded to my call to help Cary, when both of us were total strangers. Not only did she come to Cary's aid, but she also sang at her funeral, extending a further sense of peace to Cary's family and friends. Her voice was bright, lyrical, and joyous, in direct contrast to conventional funeral gloom. The effect was hard to analyze. Perhaps it was because Grace did not believe in death, and her songs somehow transcended it.

Several weeks later, Grace called me. She had just finished reading a book I had written about a young Sherpa from the Himalayas whom we had brought back to this country for medical treatment that he could not get in Nepal. She apparently liked the way it was written because she said to me, "Liz, I want to ask you something."

"Sure, Grace," I said. "I've asked an awful lot of you."

"Many people have asked me to have my story told. My full life story, I guess. I loved reading your book. Would you be willing to write mine?"

I told Grace that I was more than flattered that she chose me, but that I was not the right person to do the job. She needed to find a religious writer, someone who was conversant with the Bible. Grace disagreed. That was exactly what she wanted to avoid, she said. She wanted her story to be told completely objectively, not for the religious market but for the wide public. She wanted to avoid any proselytizing or preachiness. And I was the right person, she was sure of that.

Before I had a chance to decline, Grace asked if we could get together and talk informally about the possibility. If I still didn't want to do it after that, she would understand. I agreed.

Actually, I was quite curious to learn how she had

discovered her healing ability. And I was really curious about her personal life. I knew that she was married and had four children, but I still had a hard time imagining Grace whipping up peanut butter sandwiches from nine to five and then performing miracles from seven to eleven. After Grace went through her appointment book, juggling her tight July schedule, we decided on the following Friday at noon. My curiosity was about to be satisfied.

Over lunch Grace began talking about her life. As the afternoon wore on, I became convinced that Grace had an incredible story and that perhaps I could tell it. But everything would hinge on credibility. Who would believe it? I had a hard time believing it myself. Could her charisma and strange powers be conveyed on the printed page? Could I avoid writing a book that turned out to be just another "Jesus freak" story? Could I confirm those healings that had taken place so that I or a skeptic would believe them? Could I avoid writing the type of book that drips with syrup and sentimentality?

When I expressed these doubts to Grace, she said that I would be free to speculate about the plus and minus points of her life and the ministry. She would cooperate fully, providing me with names and telephone numbers of those who had been healed. She would also supply doctors' affidavits and everything else she had records of. I would have complete access to her files and would be free to conduct interviews at all the services. She would even welcome it if I could persuade medical doctors to come to the services and observe.

Over the next several weeks, I attended every possible service, watching Grace performing, looking for false notes, analyzing her audiences, witnessing the hundreds of people literally collapsing on the floor from her touch.

Then, over a twelve-month span of time, I pieced Grace's life together. Because of her hectic schedule, including services every Friday, Saturday, and Sunday, counselings every Wednesday, and a full office routine in between, this wasn't easy. But we managed. Sometimes the interviews were at my house in Weston, a forty-five-minute drive from Grace's home and office near Danbury. Or sometimes I would drive up there for the afternoon. There were also times when Grace and I would meet halfway. I'd park my car at the A&P, get into hers (I always got into Grace's car, even though she has a slightly heavy foot, because she likes to drive), and head thirty miles south to White Plains, where her mother lives in a large, modern senior-citizen complex only blocks from the Projects, where she had raised her three children.

On the way back, Grace would wind up and down the treeless streets of her old neighborhood, stopping every block or so to point out Mount Carmel Church, where she sang her first solo; St. John's parochial school, which she, her brother, and her sister had attended free of tuition because their mother was blind and unable to walk them to the bus stop for the bus to the public school; the Ranch House movie theater, where they had sometimes gone on Saturdays; and Shelley's Restaurant, where on very special occasions, the three children would all share one ten-cent ice cream sundae.

Finally, after twenty two-hour cassette tapings and scores of phone calls to Grace and those who have known her, I was able to reconstruct Grace's life—a life that didn't exactly parallel that of Rebecca of Sunnybrook Farm. It was more like the Coal Miner's Daughter with a bit of Oliver Twist thrown in.

CHAPTER THREE 🌺🌺

At the time when Grace was born, her mother and father were living in two and a half rooms above a bar on North Lexington Avenue in the center of White Plains, New York. It was in the part of town where police preferred to patrol after dark with partners. Across the street from the rented rooms was the fire station, and two blocks down, the railroad station. To muffle the sounds of clanging fire bells and strident train whistles, Grace's mother would stuff rags between the cracks in the window frame. That also kept the draft down to a minimum in the winter. In the summer, they chose the noise over the heat.

Antoinette Tskanikas, a comely, agreeable woman in her late twenties, passed the days caring for her three small children, Grace, Cecelia, and baby James. Her failing eyesight no longer allowed her to pursue her favorite pastime, reading. Even the large newspaper's print was blurred. It would only be a matter of years before retinitis pigmentosa rendered her totally blind. For entertainment, she listened to *Amos 'n Andy, The*

Lone Ranger, Jack Benny, or anything else that would keep her from thinking too much about what her husband George was up to.

George Tskanikas, or "George the Greek" as he was better known down at the Owampum Street pool hall and at the Hamilton Street police station, kept office hours determined strictly by how many people he could hustle out of their money. His specialty was cards, his subspecialty, pool and various misdemeanors that would occasionally get him hauled away in the paddy wagon.

When George was on a winning roll, he stayed away for three or four days. When he returned home, however, he did not come empty handed. One time, on a Good Friday, he brought a two-inch sirloin steak that a waiter friend from a Greek restaurant had slipped him out the kitchen door for a dollar. Antoinette sat the three small children down to the first piece of meat they had had in weeks. But she herself would not partake of the feast, protesting that it was not right for Catholic adults to eat meat on Good Friday, or any other Friday, for that matter. That sent George into a rage. With a sweep of his arm, he sent the entire meal onto the kitchen floor. "Anytime you have a steak on the table, it's a Good Friday!" he thundered. James, as hungry as a puppy dog, ate the meat from the floor.

Another time when George was in a good mood, he stole a dog for his favorite daughter, Grace. "Every kid should have a dog," he said, dragging the reluctant mutt into the sparse living room. As soon as George took off again, Antoinette returned the dog to its owners just down the road.

But when George was losing, he was at his worst. "Greeks don't lose!" he would holler as he threw the door open, pushed his five-foot-nine-inch solid frame

29

past his wife, and headed toward the bedroom, where the children were sleeping. Taking his belt off, he would strike wildly at Grace. Antoinette would plead with him to stop beating her.

"I'll stop lickin' her," he shouted, "when she stops cryin'!" But that would not make Grace stop crying. It had the reverse effect; it made her cry louder and longer in an attempt to wear her enraged father out, sparing her younger sister and baby brother from the thick, flailing strap.

The love Antoinette had once had for George faded with each violent incident. Now only compassion was left for the man she had married—the man her father had warned from the beginning was a bum and not worthy of his favorite child.

Antoinette deserved better. She was the first in the Buetti family to graduate from high school. And she graduated at the top of her class. Before she married, when Antoinette wasn't helping out in her father's corner grocery store she was writing poetry and short stories and reading the classics. "One day I'm going to be a writer, Daddy!" she would call across to her father, Nicola Buetti, at the meat counter, wedged between huge slabs of beef and pork.

"Forget that nonsense and weigh vegetables!" he would playfully call back in a thick Italian accent. "My little girl's gonna grow up and marry on the other side of town. She not-a have to work."

For Nicola, the "other side of town" was where the sons of the doctors and lawyers lived in sprawling country estates, complete with carriage houses and stables. But that wasn't in the stars for Antoinette. At nineteen she met George Tskanikas at an amusement park, and they were married a year later.

The thought of packing up Grace, Cecelia, and James and leaving George crossed Antoinette's mind many times. But when reality set in, she felt powerless. Where does a nearly sightless, penniless woman with three small children go to escape? She couldn't go back home to her parents—her pride wouldn't allow for that. Besides, in the last few years Nicola had been ill and had been forced to sell the grocery store that he and his wife, Annuzzata, had worked so hard for all their lives, in order to pay the medical bills and living expenses.

It would be bad enough, Antoinette thought, to be Italian, Catholic, and divorced; add to that being nearly blind, and the state might view her as an unfit mother and take her children away. At least now they did have a roof over their heads, even though at regular intervals the gas and electricity were shut off. And no one was starving. Antoinette always managed to have a meal on the table every evening.

If George gave Antoinette a dollar, she and the children walked down North Lexington Avenue, past St. John's Church, to the A&P on Central Avenue. There she would buy fifty pounds of potatoes for fifty cents and three pounds of onions for a dime. The remaining forty cents would go into a special hiding place for the weeks when George wasn't lucky. Placing the bags into the folding carriage, they walked home hand in hand, with Grace cheerfully pushing a week's worth of suppers.

"Things are going to get real good, Mommy," six-year-old Grace would say after each beating or whenever she noticed her mother getting quiet.

"I know that, honey," Grace's mother would answer, not wanting to destroy her daughter's faith. But Antoinette did worry about the effect the beatings were

31

having on her little girl. Was Grace retreating from the real world when she went into the bedroom, fell down to her hands and knees, and talked to Jesus as if he were right there with her?

"Daddy didn't mean to give me that lickin', Jesus," Antoinette would hear her say. Was this normal behavior? Did Grace say anything about the beatings at school? Did the nuns tell her to pray like that? Or was it George's mother, Vacelia Tskanikas, who after having eleven children left her husband and became a nun in the Greek Orthodox Church?

Whatever it was that influenced Grace to spend so much time praying had to be healthier than what was influencing James. He too was withdrawing, but he had no such outlet. At least Grace had Jesus; James didn't even have his toy truck anymore. The Salvation Army had given the children each a toy: Grace got a doll carriage, Cecelia a doll, and James a truck. But when George came home after a three-day losing streak and saw the shiny red truck that James was pushing along the floor, he jumped on it and smashed it to pieces, just because he had never had a truck when he was a little boy.

At times like this, it was hard for Antoinette to have compassion for George. She had to constantly remind herself that he couldn't help himself. He himself had been a product of child abuse in the old Greek style. Violence was the only way he knew to cope with frustration, anger, disappointment, and anything in life that wasn't picture perfect. His own father, Dymetrios Tskanikas, a Greek immigrant, had beat his eleven children as part of a daily routine, reason or no reason. He would tie George and his brothers up in the basement of their Yonkers home and whip them with a belt buckle. Sometimes he would refuse them food, and George and his brothers were forced to eat dirt off the basement floor in a meager attempt to ward off hunger pangs.

Although Dymetrios—Grace's grandfather—was a hat cleaner, he rarely brought home a paycheck. If his pay wasn't gambled away, it would be squandered on women of the evening. When he did bring money home, he would give his wife Vacelia only one dollar at a time, telling her to "make do." There was no way, even in those days, to feed a family on an occasional dollar, so Vacelia took in sewing from the factories in and around Yonkers. She was fast and adept with her fingers and was told by more than one factory foreman that she could do the work of three women, and do it better.

Fortunately, as the family grew, the older children could take care of the younger ones, so their mother was able to spend practically every waking moment sewing. Vacelia, a devoutly religious woman, had three goals: to earn enough to pay the bills, to save enough to do without Dymetrios's stipend and, finally, to follow a religious calling to become a nun, foreshadowing her granddaughter Grace's religious calling many years later.

Two years after their eleventh child was born, Vacelia was ordained a Greek Orthodox nun by the archbishop. With a heavy black habit and a huge crucifix draped around her neck, she went out into the streets collecting donations for the Church, which permitted nuns to live with their families. In the evening she went back home to take care of the children, who still lived with her. Dymetrios was never seen or heard from again.

It was almost inevitable that Grace's father, George, would follow the same pattern as his father.

Even when George made an effort to do something

33

tender, he could never pull it off. One of the most graphic examples, vividly recalled by Grace years later, occurred when she was six years old. Her father had taken them to Coney Island beach for the day. It was the first time they had ever been to a beach and they took a special picnic lunch that their mother had prepared. Ninety percent blind by this time, Antoinette had decided to stay home. She was not yet used to coping with large crowds.

It was a perfect day, hot, with a cool breeze sweeping in from the Atlantic and across the children as they scooped sand into pans for their sand castles. In between turret and moat construction, George raced Cecelia and James out into the water, and as they screeched with joy, he lobbed them one by one, or sometimes two at a time, into the saltwater waves. Then the two would run back into their father's arms, begging for just one more toss. Grace, however, did not like the water. She was content to run back and forth just to the very edge of the water, filling up pots for the castle, and watching her brother and sister from a safe distance.

But George had other ideas. He thought that Grace should be made to be unafraid of the water. He swung the screaming curly-haired child onto his shoulders and ran down the crowded beach and into the ocean. The more Grace pleaded with him to stop, the farther he splashed through the waves. When he was neck deep, he gave Grace an ultimatum: Stop crying, or get dunked. Grace could not stop crying. George, a man of his word, dunked her, not once but repeatedly. She stopped crying, finally. She almost stopped breathing as well. George carried her back to the beach, where she threw up the salt water and her lunch.

That incident was the last time the children were ever left alone with George. He couldn't be trusted. When Antoinette went for her weekly classes to learn Braille, Vacelia, George's mother—whom everyone called "Yaya," the Greek word for grandmother—would now babysit. Those times were special for everyone. Grace, Cecelia, and James would wait anxiously at the Hamilton Street bus stop for the jovial, heavyset Yaya. She always brought with her a large grocery bag stuffed with enough food to get the family through to her next week's visit. As they walked toward home, she would allow her grandchildren to rummage through it.

Although Yaya loved all her grandchildren, she seemed to have a special affinity for Grace, almost as if there were an unspoken bond between them. While James and Cecelia jumped rope and played stickball with the other kids on the street, Grace and Yaya sat on the front stoop and talked about Jesus. Grace never tired of hearing how He had walked the earth two thousand years earlier, healing and helping everyone He came in contact with. Yaya, who had a knack for drama, could repeat complete passages from the New Testament with fervor that made ancient history sound as if it were a news flash.

During these visits, Grace told Yaya about the nightly conversations she had with Jesus. With Yaya's thick, scratchy fingers wrapped around her granddaughter's delicate hand, Grace would tell all about how Jesus protected her when her father beat her. "Jesus stops Daddy's strap from hurting me," Grace would say, adding that even when she didn't have time to put the pillow between her and the blanket, she still didn't feel a thing. "Jesus promised me that Daddy's going to stop going to Owampum Street pool hall. And that one day, if I keep praying real hard, he's going to get Jesus in his heart too."

Yaya listened to every word of what her young granddaughter told her, not doubting for a moment that it would come true. The Lord kept his promises, Yaya was certain of that. After all, He had promised Yaya that someday she would collect enough donations to build a neighborhood church so that all the old people and the very young would not have to go far to worship. And in the last few years that had come true. Yaya had scraped together enough money to build a Greek Orthodox church. The small unassuming structure sat at 106 Holland Avenue in White Plains, under the auspices of the archbishop and the direct supervision of Vacelia Tskanikas—Yaya.

Shortly after Yaya built the church, her son George laid down a rule: His wife and children were not permitted to go into his mother's church. They were also forbidden to go into St. John's, or any other church. He was not going to have his wife and three children turn into a bunch of religious fanatics the way his mother had after a door-to-door salesman had sold her a Bible. His family was going to be normal.

That house rule was easily circumvented. George was rarely, if ever, home on Sundays. Furthermore, whenever he was home he was sleeping off booze and his gambling spree. He would never know that his family had slipped off to Sunday mass. Antoinette was still cautious, however. She made certain that they heard mass from the vestibule. That way if one of the kids, who had the door staked out, spotted George coming, they could make a quick getaway and not be trapped in a pew.

By Grace's tenth birthday, George was staying away

longer than his usual three or four days. Sometimes the family wouldn't see him from week to week, and Antoinette would have no idea where he was. During these times, she would fear that George had gotten himself into trouble, real trouble. Months earlier, police had raided the pool hall and loaded George and thirty-one others into the back of a paddy wagon. But George was home the next day and back at the pool hall that night.

The day Antoinette announced that her eye doctor wanted George to come for a consultation, he left in a rage, and she thought he might never return.

"George," Antoinette said, "Dr. Suzansky wants you to come with me on my next visit."

"What does he gotta see me for?" George said, leaning over the kitchen sink shaving. He was getting dressed to go to a new job as a short-order cook. It would be his first legitimate position.

Antoinette knew exactly why her doctor wanted to see George. He wanted to impress upon her husband how important it was for him to spend all his free time with her. He wanted George to take her to the park so that she could study the trees and look at the flowers. He wanted her to go to art museums and see beautiful paintings. He wanted her to go to as many places and to see as many things as possible, because soon, such sights would only be memories.

"I think it'll only be a few months now before all my sight is gone. Maybe the doctor wants to talk to you about—"

George didn't let her finish. "You guinea," he shouted, "you can't see nights. Now you're sayin' you can't see days neither! What good are you to me?"

He threw his razor into the sink, went into the bedroom, grabbed extra clothes, stuffed them into his old

37

army satchel, and left. Three months later, they were divorced.

Fortunately, before the divorce was finalized, Antoinette heard that only a few miles from where they lived, low-cost housing was in the process of being completed. Veterans would have first choice. This meant two things: George would qualify since he had been in the army; and since the divorce was still pending, he could sign up so that his children would have a decent place to live. George agreed to this. Within months, Antoinette and the three children moved into the spanking-new apartment complex known as the Projects.

Grace and Cecelia were ecstatic. They not only had a bedroom for just the two of them, they had a closet too. James had his own bedroom, as did Antoinette. But the best part was that for the first time in the children's lives, there was a bathroom inside the apartment. No longer did they have to go out into a musty hallway to share a toilet with two other families. No longer did they have to bathe in a large metal tub that sat near the kitchen sink.

The rent for the new apartment came to $39.50 a month. The court ordered George to pay his wife eighty percent of his sixty-dollar-a-week income and to drop the alimony off at the city hall for Antoinette to collect later. He was not permitted to visit the apartment. If he wanted to see his children, he could meet them outside the building on Saturday to take them to a matinee or for an ice cream sundae. They were not allowed to go where he lived. After a year of irregular Saturday visits, George gradually stopped seeing his children altogether.

Life was easier with George gone. The support payments were on time. The Projects, five huge buildings that each housed ninety families, was a safe place to live. It had a small-city atmosphere, where everyone was friendly and helpful.

As the months slipped into years, Antoinette never stopped thanking God that her children were growing into conscientious adults. It could have gone the other way, especially for Grace, who had received the brunt of her father's behavior. But it didn't. Grace was blossoming into a beautiful and talented young woman.

Although Antoinette, blind now for three years, was unable to see the physical transformation in her daughter, she was able to hear—along with half the people in the Projects—that Grace was a gifted singer. Grace's voice came as no big surprise to Antoinette. At three months, she had been cooing "Rock-a-Bye-Baby." And at a year, she could sing complete songs along with her mother.

Now, everywhere they went, someone would inevitably ask Grace to sing something. Grace didn't need any coaxing. For the Irish traffic cop on the corner, she would let loose with his favorite, "Tura-Lura-Lura." For Father Dunn, it was "Ave Maria." And for Sister Neary, "On This Day, Oh Beautiful Mother." Her brother James's favorite was "Don't Step on My Blue Suede Shoes," but Grace had a hard time remembering rock 'n roll, and after the first several verses she would segue into an upbeat gospel number.

Grace's faith intensified after her father left. "Jesus promised," Grace would tell her mother, "that one day, while I'm singing to God, Daddy's going to come back to me. And to Jesus too."

Antoinette never encouraged her daughter to believe

that. She doubted very much if they would ever see him again. Through George's mother, Antoinette learned that he had remarried. This, Antoinette thought, made it even more unlikely that he would want to see Grace, Cecelia, and James.

Cecelia and James rarely talked abut their father; it was always Grace who brought him up. Usually after she had been praying, she would say that one day they'd all be with their "earthly" father again—after George left, that was the way she referred to him.

At thirteen, Grace was stricken with a serious viral attack. Antoinette called the family doctor, who came to their apartment and gave Grace a penicillin injection. Shortly after he left, Grace got out of bed to go to the bathroom. As she did, her legs crumbled and she fell forward into an open closet.

Antoinette heard her scream. She ran to the closet, where Grace was lying on the floor.

"Mommy, I think I'm dying," Grace groaned. She was clutching her throat and moaning.

Antoinette ran to the phone and called the doctor's office. Miraculously, she reached him, and he returned within fifteen minutes. Recognizing that Grace was in anaphylactic shock, he gave her an injection of Adrenalin. Her breathing stabilized, but she was barely conscious.

She lay in bed, almost paralyzed, for over three weeks, her swollen joints immobilizing her with what is medically known as "serum sickness."

One night, she awoke suddenly and looked at the foot of her bed. The whole area seemed to be brilliantly illuminated. In the center, she saw the full figure of

Jesus, his arms outstretched, looking at her. His countenance reflected beauty and serenity.

She heard the vision say clearly, "Come to me. Don't be afraid. You are healed."

Grace found herself getting out of bed, her pain and paralysis gone. As the figure disappeared, she was flooded with a sense of joy and dedication. Christ had become more real to her than ever.

By Grace's sixteenth birthday, she was ready for a major change. With her mother's mixed blessing, she left St. John's School and transferred to White Plains High School. Grace had had enough of the math, science, and other academic courses that were required at the parochial school. She told her mother that she wasn't going to become an accountant or a brain surgeon, so there was no reason to put herself through the torture of nearly flunking those subjects every semester. The public school, on the other hand, offered a business course in which she could take typing and shorthand.

At first her mother argued against the idea. She reminded Grace that she would be starting all over again at a school where she knew no one, a school more than three times as large as St. John's. She would simply be lost in the crowd. But Grace was adamant.

Once the decision had been made, Antoinette rationalized that it was probably all for the better. Grace had been spending too much time with the choir. But within weeks of starting the new school, Grace joined the high school choir. And within two short months, she was singled out to sing two solos for the Christmas pageant.

Six months later, she was booked to sing at the Westchester County Center in White Plains for a benefit starring John Forsythe and Leslie Uggams. Wearing a red chiffon floor-length gown, Grace belted out "Faith, Hope and Charity" and "It's Almost Tomorrow" to over five thousand cheering people. While shouts of "bravo" rang through the evening air at the County Center, Grace was cued to sing an encore. Confused, nervous, and euphoric, she sang "Oh, What a Beautiful Morning" at just a few minutes past midnight, and she received a standing ovation. Later, she received an offer for a full scholarship to the Juilliard School of Music.

With two years of high school left, Grace didn't have to make any immediate commitments. Her mother was glad of that: She would have her junior and senior year to get singing out of her system and to get on with the business course so that she would never have to be dependent on a man. But after only one semester of typing and shorthand, Grace was bored to death. There was no way she wanted to spend forty hours a week plunking at typewriter keys and scribbling shorthand in a stuffy office building after graduation. Her worst fear was that she would waste precious years doing something she didn't like. Grace had never been one to waste time doing things she didn't want to do. Even at sixteen, this rule extended to her social life.

Grace was popular at school; she had attained that popularity by standing aside, but not aloof, from the crowd. Her friends recognized that she appeared to have special powers. Ever since Grace could remember, she seemed to know things about people that she couldn't reasonably be expected to know. Today, some might call this extrasensory perception, or ESP. But Grace had never heard of ESP, and even if she had, she wouldn't have attributed her abilities to that. She believed they came from Jesus. Her public high school friends didn't know what to believe. Some thought that maybe it was because she had gone to St. John's, a Catholic school, for so many years. Others wondered if her insights grew from those of her blind mother. And still others thought that it might have something to do with the fact that she had a grandmother who was a nun. But whatever the source, her classmates all had to agree that whenever Grace prayed and then gave advice, there always seemed to be a successful outcome.

Some of her premonitions were vividly dramatic. One incident happened on a crisp fall evening following a football game. Everyone's spirits were up. White Plains High had just upset their chief rival. The usual protocol for after-game festivities was for over a dozen kids to pile into a car, hopefully a convertible (the top would be down regardless of the weather), and head anywhere—fast.

Grace and four of her friends broke with protocol. Their celebration was going to be at Grace's apartment, where her mother was waiting with a giant bowl of hot buttered popcorn and soft drinks. While they were heading toward the Projects, a Chevy convertible overflowing with schoolmates pulled up beside them. "Jump in!" they shouted to the girls.

Grace and her four friends stopped and chatted briefly, explaining that they had other plans. Then the girls continued toward home. The driver of the car cruised his Chevy slowly beside them, and he and the others pleaded with the five attractive girls to hop in.

After two blocks of coaxing, Grace's friends gave in. As Grace stood watching all four of them squeeze into the overloaded back seat, a sickening feeling overcame her. It was as if someone had punched her in the stomach, knocking the wind from her. For reasons she couldn't explain, she shouted above the car's blasting radio for her friends to get out. Thinking that Grace was just being a stick-in-the-mud, her friends called back for her to get in and join them. Within moments, that sick feeling intensified. Suddenly Grace interpreted it as a warning that something terrible was about to happen.

They kept calling for Grace to get in. And she did, but only long enough to bodily drag two of her friends out; one she pulled by the hair. Before she was able to get the other two out, the driver peeled away, leaving behind screeching rubber and the fading shrieks of football cheers.

The next morning Grace awoke to the news: The driver had wrapped the car around a tree. There were many injured. Her two friends were dead.

CHAPTER FOUR 🌱🌱

IN GRACE'S FINAL YEAR OF HIGH SCHOOL, SHE made a decision. Two months before summer vacation, she walked into her high school counselor's office and turned down the full scholarship to the Juilliard School of Music in New York City. This decision had not come easily; it had caused her months of anguish. She was well aware that a degree from Juilliard would be a ticket to a musical career. But she also knew the emotional burden it would put on her blind mother. As the replacement for her father as head of the family, Grace would be sorely missed. And she would have a long, arduous commute to New York City. The scholarship did not include travel expenses. Where were they going to get an additional thirty dollars a month?

As a meager substitute for Juilliard, Grace enrolled at Wynn's Beauty Culture School on Main Street in White Plains, only blocks from where she lived in the Projects. The school had a program whereby she could work her way through the twelve-month course without putting any money up front.

But the main reason Grace decided on beauty school was her favorite aunt, Grace, for whom she had been named. Aunt Grace was a hairdresser in the Bronx. On Saturdays, young Grace would often go to the shop that her aunt owned and lend a hand shampooing hair, sweeping the floor, or carrying out whatever odd jobs had to be done. Grace loved to watch her aunt create the large bouffant styles of the sixties and join in the animated conversation of the shop. Her aunt had a way of bringing out the humorous side of everyone, even old Mrs. Kiasky, who specialized in stories of funerals and chronic illness. Five minutes after Aunt Grace had begun to finger-wave Mrs. Kiasky's sparse gray hair, even the old lady would smile.

The day Grace registered for beauty school, she consoled herself with those memories. Wynn's Beauty Culture School might not be as glamorous as the Juilliard School of Music, she thought, but it wouldn't be as dull as typing and filing in a stuffy office. If she worked in a hair salon, she could relate to the customers the way her aunt always did. And if she felt like breaking out into a song, she could do that too. At least, nobody had ever minded at her aunt's shop. Everyone always requested her favorite numbers. Mrs. Kiasky's favorite was "You'll Never Walk Alone." She told Grace she wanted her to sing it at her funeral.

The next time Grace sang "You'll Never Walk Alone," however, was not at Mrs. Kiasky's funeral but at a beauty contest sponsored by the Knights of Columbus at which Grace was a contestant. Although Grace didn't win the title, she was one of five finalists out of forty-seven chosen from Westchester County. As Grace's mother sat in the audience at the Knights of Columbus Hall listening to her daughter's crystal-clear voice, everything inside her said that Grace was destined for a musical career, Juilliard or no Juilliard.

By the time Grace reached her twentieth birthday, she had received her beautician's license and was working in a salon in White Plains. She continued to sing in the church choir and to go to two masses every Sunday to pray, especially for her father, and to be guided in the right direction according to God's will.

Within a year, Grace returned to the Knights of Columbus Hall for another very special event: her wedding reception to celebrate her marriage to Larry DiBicarri, whom she had met through friends two years earlier.

Grace had never planned to marry at twenty. But after meeting Larry, she had a change of heart. He was different from the other boys she had known. He seemed to share the same sort of love for God, and for children too. Grace had recognized that quality the first time he came to pick her up for a date.

Although Antoinette couldn't see Larry frolic with the neighborhood children each time he came to visit, she could perceive his gentle nature through their gaiety whenever he was around. She "saw" his boyish smile and deep brown eyes every time he came through the door, gave her a peck on the cheek, and wanted to know if he could get her something from the store.

"Blind people and children are the best judges of character," Antoinette told Grace the evening she came home wearing a diamond engagement ring. "I never wanted you to marry so young," she said, "but that was before I knew Larry."

With Antoinette's blessing, Grace walked down the aisle of St. John's Church one warm June morning. Bill Tskanikas, her father's brother, gave her away as the choir sang "Our Father." Later, everyone was invited to the reception for a buffet that included everything from roast beef to ravioli to a three-tier wedding cake. To add to the gaiety, a four-piece band played.

At one point, Uncle Bill led the guests in an exuberant Greek dance. Not to be outdone, Antoinette did the tarantella, an Italian folk dance.

"Not to forget the Buetti half!" Antoinette called out as she joined hands between her new son-in-law and daughter and began to dance in a huge circle of over two hundred guests.

But in spite of the mirth, there was sadness. Grace's heart was not as light as her steps. She missed her father. And she missed him more on this wedding day than at any time in her life. As she danced in the circle, clutching her mother's hand in her left and her uncle's in her right, she had to resist tears.

Earlier in the day, her emotions had gotten the best of her. It was just before they left for the church. Her mother was snapping the back of her gown. Her aunt was standing on the bed arranging the delicate lace veil onto her freshly coiffeured hairdo.

"Grace looks just like a fairy princess!" whispered two little flower girls as they peeked into the bedroom.

"If I ever wanted my eyesight, it's now," Antoinette said, holding Grace to her. "To see my baby girl walk down that aisle."

Grace looked at herself in the full-length mirror. She didn't feel like a fairy princess. And she didn't feel like a bride. She felt incomplete without her father there to give her away.

"Flower girls, bridesmaids, and bride!" called Uncle Bill from the living room. "We gotta get the show on the road!"

Grace excused herself. She went into the bathroom and cried. All her perfectly applied eyeliner and mascara ran in streaks. This is supposed to be the happiest day of my life, she thought. And here I am sobbing in the bathroom. My father should be giving me away. Although she loved Uncle Bill, it wasn't the same. Grace tortured herself with the memory of a girlfriend's wedding a few months earlier. She remembered how Mary Ann's father had walked his daughter down the aisle. She remembered the looks on both of their faces as he gave her away. And she remembered most clearly how Mary Ann's father had had tears in his eyes as he returned to his seat alone. Later he had told Grace that the only thing that had kept him from breaking down altogether was the comforting thought that soon he would have grandchildren to bounce on his knee.

The party went on well past midnight, but the bride and groom slipped away when the band stopped playing. Larry and Grace wanted to get a few hours' rest before the nine-hour drive south to Virginia Beach. There they spent their honeymoon.

Ten days later, they returned to New York and moved into an attic apartment in White Plains. Once settled, they began their life as a young married couple. Larry had a promising career with General Electric. Only weeks after he had received his diploma from Westchester County Business School, he was hired as a machine technician. His starting salary was sixty-two dollars a week, nearly twenty dollars less than what Grace earned. But by the end of the year, he had received a promotion and a raise.

The money could not have come at a better time. Eleven months after they were married, Grace gave birth to Larry, Junior. The following year, their second son, Christopher, was born. Ten months after that, twin daughters, Sharon and Karen, arrived. In three and a half years, they had four children and enough debts to force Larry to moonlight at two extra jobs: at night he worked at the post office, and on weekends, he did landscaping with his uncle.

Larry didn't mind the work, but he did mind the amount of time it kept him away from his family. However, he had to be realistic. His goal was to save enough money to buy a house in Connecticut with a backyard big enough for a swingset, a sandbox, and a dog.

Grace had eased into the role of mother of four with little trouble. Ten years of babysitting in the Projects had equipped her well. But three pregnancies in less than four years brought on a serious problem with varicose veins. With her last pregnancy, her doctor warned that a slight injury to the area could cause serious bleeding. Phlebitis was also a danger.

Six months after the twins were born, the condition showed no signs of improvement. It was just the opposite. She could remain standing for only minutes at a time. This was not easy with four children scampering in all directions twelve hours a day. The doctor informed Grace that he had no alternative but to suggest surgery to correct the condition. Grace took his advice and checked into the hospital. Friends and relatives helped out by taking care of the children. Larry took two days off from work without pay so that he could be with Grace during visiting hours.

However, all did not go as planned. The operation was a success, but the aftermath was a disaster. In the hours following the surgery, Grace received an injection of morphine. No one, including Grace, was aware that she was allergic to the drug. If morphine is given to someone highly allergic, the results are often fatal.

"Within minutes of receiving the shot," Grace recalled, "I began to have difficulty in breathing. A rash broke out over my body. 'I don't feel well,' I told an elderly man who had been in the room visiting. He was a patient from across the hall. When the man noticed the rash suddenly appear, he took off in search of a doctor or nurse.

"While he was away, my throat began to close. I began to panic. I couldn't scream for help. I couldn't get out of bed. Both of my legs were wound in bandages. It was impossible to move. In an effort to attract attention, I knocked the phone off its stand. Still no one came.

"The last thing I remember was the doctor coming into the room. He was shouting something about circulatory collapse and getting Adrenalin into me right away. Suddenly I felt my consciousness slipping away. Then the panic had dissolved into a type of tranquillity I had never experienced before. My body became feather light. There was no pain. I felt myself rising above my physical body on the hospital bed. But there was no fear.

"I heard chamber music begin to play. I felt as if I were on my way toward a white mountain peak. Once I arrived at the peak, I looked below. There were clouds. Above was a bright light. Everything around that bright light was illuminated. It seemed to be coming from behind a golden gate. But it wasn't an ordinary gold. It had a lustre that I had never seen before. I wanted to go through the gate. I was convinced that I would see my aunt Grace, who had died several years earlier.

"Suddenly a powerful light shone behind the gate. I

knew Jesus was the light behind that gate. It illuminated everything. I felt compelled to go toward it. There was perfect peace. But I felt a tug and heard a voice that said it wasn't my time. I had to go back. I felt myself descending in the same manner as I had ascended to the mountain peak. Gently I floated back down, and joined up with my physical body. When I opened my eyes, I was back in the hospital bed. There was a nurse, doctor, nun, and the elderly man in my room. The man was crying that I was too young to die. The doctor simply said, 'You gave us a scare.' "

Although Grace didn't know it at the time, her experience paralleled that of hundreds of patients that Dr. Raymond Moody described in his bestseller *Life After Life.*

The experience left Grace more determined than ever to spread the word that Jesus was alive. For the next ten years, she made regular visits to the terminally ill, talking to them about Jesus and what happens at the time of death. "Death is simply passing from one form of existence to another," she would say. "You shed your physical body. But you maintain your individual awareness. Death has no sting." As concrete evidence that this was true, Grace would vividly recount her own experience, when she had moved into the next world and returned. Her faith that one day she would be with her heavenly father had grown even stronger.

As her children grew, so did Grace's ambition. On Mondays and Thursdays, after supper, she changed into jeans, a sweatshirt, and sneakers while the boys cleaned up the dinner dishes. Then she loaded her twin daughters, baseball bats, mitts, and softballs into the back of the station wagon and headed out to Memorial Park, where she coached a girls' softball team. Sports for girls were lacking in the sleepy town of Brookfield, Connecticut; recognizing that, Grace had formed the first softball team for girls only. This was months after the family had moved to Brookfield into their "dream house," a split-level ranch house that sat on a rolling two-acre lot shaded by striped awnings and eighty-foot oaks.

Grace was tireless. On Tuesday evenings she held an informal Bible study group for teenagers in her home. Many of the kids who came had been in trouble with the police. The offenses were usually minor: petty shoplifting and vandalism. Grace felt that with proper guidance and direction, further crimes could be averted. At the Bible study group, the teenagers sang with Grace. These evenings had the ambiance more of a rock concert than a Bible study group, but the beat was spirited country gospel, and all the songs were in praise of Jesus.

By the end of the first year, seventy kids were regulars. Several counselors at the high school were partly responsible for the increased attendance. They had seen the dramatic change in several of their students who had been hard-core drug addicts and alcoholics.

But all was not quiet in the valley. Several concerned parents banded together to put a stop to the "fanaticism," as they termed it in a letter to Grace. One of the most devastating complaints Grace received came from the mother of a young man whom Grace had literally picked up off her doorstep. He had been so high from drugs and alcohol that he couldn't walk. When he sobered up, Grace talked to him about Jesus, about how all-loving and forgiving He is. The boy confessed that he was actively contemplating suicide. He felt alone in the world. He was unable to talk to his parents. He felt as if nobody cared what happened to him.

Grace told the young man that Jesus cared and that

she cared too. And she invited him to come back the following week for Bible study. He did so not only that next week, but every week thereafter, that is, until he was forbidden by his mother.

"I don't know what's going on there," the mother told Grace over the phone, "but I don't like it! It isn't normal for young people to be singing religious songs and reading the Bible every week. My son has lost interest in going out with friends. He just isn't acting normal."

Grace asked the woman if she thought it was more normal to get drunk and take drugs. The woman said no, but at least that was all part of growing up. Then she warned that she would be returning "that Bible" to Grace by mail. She said that if Grace ever called the house or tried to get her son back to "one of those things," she would report her to the police.

For several months, the young man heeded his mother's warning. However, one Tuesday evening during Bible study, he arrived back on Grace's doorstep. He was in the same condition as he had been the first time they had met, drunk and stoned. Grace asked her two sons to bring him in and lay him down in the bedroom. Then Grace phoned the boy's house. She told the mother to come pick up her son.

When the mother arrived, she was shocked to see her son stumbling around the bedroom, incoherent, unable even to put on his shoes. While she waited for him to sober up, the mother sat in the kitchen. It was there that she had a change of heart. The young people she observed in the living room were joyful. There was guitar music, singing, and laughter. The most potent things being passed around were taco chips and root beer. Grace did not appear to be a fanatic. If anything, she seemed as wholesome as the teenagers, leading them in various gospel songs, reading to them from Scripture.

Mother and son came into the living room together. Tentatively, they sat down. At the end of the evening, the mother asked to be forgiven for the horrible things she had said. And she wanted to know if perhaps her son could return to the group. Grace hugged her and told her that she had been hoping she'd ask that.

The boy became one of the regulars. His mother also became a regular at the monthly parents' and children's night. Today the young man is in a seminary.

During these years, Grace also acted with the Brookfield Players and the St. Gregory Players in local theater productions, putting on benefits for various charities. She also managed to find time to organize a concert called The Black, White and Free Gospel Concert.

As the title implies, the concert was racially mixed, nondenominational, and charged no admission. Grace had been inspired to organize this concert during a time when racial tension was festering in the school system and on the streets of nearby Danbury. She feared that the riots that had recently happened in Los Angeles, Detroit, Cleveland, and other heavily populated urban areas could also happen in Danbury. Grace went to the Reverend Elder C. Brown, a prominent black religious leader in the community, and explained what she wanted to accomplish. "My aim," she told him, "is to bring people of all colors together and unite them under one God."

Reverend Brown liked the message. With his help and the help of other religious leaders, Grace eventually brought eighteen choir and folk groups from all over Connecticut together for a spring concert at Danbury High School. In an interview the day of the event, Grace told the Danbury *News-Times*, "I formed this group to show that Jesus can do the impossible. He is not limited. He can use anything or anybody He wills to bring about the evidence of His Grace. He has taken seemingly hopeless situations and turned them around. Jesus said, 'All things are possible to him who believes.' "

The turnout was far better than expected. Every seat was taken, and people were standing in the aisles and along the back of the auditorium. Grace was the official master of ceremonies. She breezed onto the stage in a flowing black and white gown, symbolic of the evening. "Lincoln freed the slaves nearly two hundred years ago," she announced, "but Jesus freed us over two thousand years ago!" There was thunderous applause, and Grace broke out with "When the Saints Go Marching In."

Grace was at home in front of an audience. Over the previous three years she had performed in her own gospel group every weekend in churches and auditoriums. But those concerts never got the attention from the press and the town officials that The Black, White and Free Gospel Concert received. Even the mayor wrote to Grace expressing his appreciation for all her efforts to unite the town of Danbury. He hoped that the concert would become an annual event. Grace wrote back, "Our God is a God of Miracles. And all things are possible through Him."

Those words were more prophetic than Grace or anyone else realized at the time. Only weeks afterward, an event would take place that would not only change Grace's life forever but would change the lives of thousands who came in contact with her.

56

Grace enjoyed the following summer as much as her kids did. She invited nine youngsters from the Projects, in shifts of three at a time, to stay with her family for a month. She took them to Kenosha Beach, on a lake a few miles from where they lived. On weekends, Larry took the boys fishing in West End Lake. On Monday and Wednesday evenings, they all went out to Memorial Park. While Grace coached the girls' softball team, Larry played touch football with the kids. Bible study continued throughout the summer, as did Grace's gospel group.

When Grace first began singing at churches and auditoriums, her only backup was a tape recorder. Now she had a drummer, two guitarists, and a bass player. They called themselves Grace 'N Vessels. Their popularity became known as far north as New Haven.

One gig was held at St. Mary's Catholic Church in Ridgefield. The turnout was expected to be over five hundred. "On a hot July evening, two weeks before the concert at St. Mary's, I came home from rehearsal," Grace recalled. "It was after midnight. I went into each of the children's bedrooms, as always. The boys were sleeping on the floor on top of their sleeping bags. Their two visiting friends from the Projects were on the bed. The covers were thrown off. The twins, Sharon and Karen, were in their room asleep in one bed. Their visiting friend was in the other bed. I arranged the fan so that it blew gently across all three girls. Then I turned and closed the door behind me.

"Larry was already asleep when I got into bed. I picked up the Bible from my nightstand and read until I felt sleepy. Then I flicked off the lamp and drifted off.

"At ten minutes after two, I was awakened by a nudge on my arm. It jolted me from a sound sleep.

Larry must have accidentally bumped me when he turned over, I thought. But seconds later, while I was awake, the same thing happened. And it wasn't Larry. Suddenly a physical and emotional presence enveloped me. I felt it was unmistakably the presence of God.

"It was that same feeling that I had experienced when I was only five years old, the time when Jesus had come to me and told me that He would not allow my earthly father to ever hurt me again. After that time, whenever my father beat me, I didn't feel a thing. The strap marks were there, but the pain wasn't. Then at ten years old, after my father had deserted the family, Jesus had come to me once again. He said that my earthly father would one day return to me and to Him.

"Now, twenty years later, I sensed that same emotional and physical presence. 'God, what is this?' I asked. I was bewildered but not afraid.

"As if out of nowhere, what sounded like bird chirpings began to flow from my lips. I didn't want to awaken Larry. I quietly went downstairs, sat down on the sofa, and began to pray. The soft, birdlike sounds continued. Within minutes, a string of long and short sounds emerged. They were like words, but they weren't English. It was more like Spanish. The long and short sounds were in rising and falling tones. Soon unintelligible sentences began forming.

"I had never experienced anything like this before. But I knew what was happening. I had been given the 'gift of tongues,' what the Bible refers to as a heavenly language—a spiritual gift. I was now convinced I was being baptized in the Holy Spirit.

"As I continued speaking in tongues, I felt God's love pour through me. I wanted to love everyone and everything. I never dreamed that I could feel so much love at one time.

" 'God, what is happening?' I said to myself. I was trying to understand why this had come upon me without warning. There were so many times I had prayed for the gift of tongues and nothing had happened.

"It was at this point that I heard God's voice for the first time. It wasn't the same as when I was a little girl. I just knew, without actually physically hearing His voice, what He was saying. It was a voice that sounded like gentle rain.

" 'Go to my people. They do not know me.'

" 'How, Lord?' I asked.

"The voice repeated, 'Sing to my people. Tell them about me.'

"I fell down to my knees. 'My Lord, my God, I will do anything you want. Send me. I'll go. I'm yours, Lord. Use me.' "

CHAPTER FIVE ❦

"S T. MARY'S INVITES YOU TO COME AND BRING your friends next Sunday evening for a lively gospel concert with Grace 'N Vessels," the notice in the church bulletin read.

Grace picked up her copy of the bulletin and tucked it inside her sundress pocket. She called to Larry, who was cutting the grass, and to the kids in the pool that she would be right back. Then she walked around the corner to visit her friend June Dimian. When Grace arrived, two other neighbors were sitting under a colorful umbrella table on the patio having iced tea.

"We'll all be there Sunday night!" one of the women called the moment she saw Grace approach.

"Then you guys won't need this," Grace said, waving the bulletin in the air.

In the previous few years, Grace's status in the neighborhood had changed dramatically. When she had first moved into the quiet development, nobody knew what to make of the attractive, energetic young mother of four who coached the first girls' softball team, was publicity chairman for Pop Warner football, ran Bible study classes for up to seventy teenagers, had a gospel group, and roller-skated up and down the street with the neighborhood kids, saying hi and waving to everybody, even to those who lived in homes much more lavish then her own—Grace was not intimidated by wealth; her bright smile and cheery greetings cut across all social barriers.

"Grace," June said, pouring iced tea, "I was telling Ann and Virginia what happened to your son last month."

Grace hesitated before answering. What had happened was so strange that few people believed it. Even Grace had a hard time accepting it. With a certain amount of reservation, she told the women that her son, Christopher, had been injured on a skateboard. She had taken him over to see Dr. William Sinton at the Danbury Orthopedics Association. The X-rays showed that Christopher had broken his collarbone. A short time later, he began to suffer from a lot of pain and had trouble getting to sleep. Grace went into his bedroom and began praying with him. As they were praying, Christopher suddenly called out that two angels had come into the room.

"Mommy, Jesus sent them to fix my collarbone."

Grace's initial reaction was to feel his forehead to check for a high temperature. She thought that perhaps a fever had combined with the pain to cause him to hallucinate. It was not in her son's character to talk about seeing angels. But as Christopher kept insisting that he had seen the angels and that the shoulder pain had disappeared, Grace recalled her own past experiences. The visions she had had as a child had been as real to her as her son's vision of angels was to him.

"There's no more pain!" the eleven-year-old shouted. He moved his shoulder up and down. He insisted on taking off the collar brace and sling.

The next day, Grace took her son back to Dr. Sinton. The set of X-rays that he took then showed that the collarbone was completely healed.

"Those angels did a good job," Dr. Sinton told Christopher. "It normally takes six to eight weeks to heal a broken collarbone. Yours healed in a fraction of that time."

He handed Christopher the brace and sling. "Here's a souvenir," he said.

Just as the neighbors were getting used to Grace's offbeat lifestyle, she came along with this one. In the quiet suburbs, you don't sit around talking about miracles and expect to maintain any sort of social standing. Ann and Virginia exchanged glances. They had grown very fond of Grace. They were charmed by her and wanted to protect her from herself. As far as they themselves were concerned, Grace was entitled to have some quirks; she did more for the young people in town than anyone. But if word spread about this purported miracle, complete with angels, they feared that others would make life uncomfortable for Grace and her family.

A polite length of time after Grace had finished her story, Ann and Virginia excused themselves, saying that their families would be wondering where dinner was. June knew exactly what her friends thought of Grace's "miracle healing." She had noticed their expressions while Grace was talking. June had to admit that the story was a hard one to swallow. However, she had been at Grace's house the day Chrisopher had come home from the doctor wearing a brace and sling. And three weeks later she had seen him playing as if nothing had happened.

But even if June hadn't seen what happened to Christopher, she still would have believed Grace. They had been friends for years. During that time, Grace had never given her any reason to distrust her.

Now, as Grace and June carried the empty pitcher and glasses from the patio back into the kitchen, June's mind shifted to an experience she had had a week earlier.

"You know, Grace," she said, splashing water into the tall narrow glasses, "after I gave my life to God last week, I feel so different. It's a good feeling, a great feeling. But in the last few days, I've developed a sudden fear that I'll wake up one morning and that peaceful feeling might be gone. It might be just all too good to be true."

"I sensed you had fear," Grace said, drying the glasses. "That's why I walked over."

Grace tossed the towel onto the countertop and went into June's bedroom. She came back with the Bible.

"It says right here in Hebrews thirteen, verse five, 'I will never leave you nor forsake you.' "

Grace took both of June's hands. "Perfect love of God casts out all fear," she said. And they began to pray that June's fear would leave.

Then suddenly and without any warning, June's eyes started to flutter. She stumbled backward two steps. Her knees buckled. She crumbled and landed on the floor. She looked as if she had been knocked unconscious. Grace was shocked; she had no idea what had happened to her friend. She had never seen anything like this before. Grace wrapped a towel around some ice cubes and was about to apply it to June's forehead when June began to mumble incoherent words. Within minutes, the slurred speech had escalated to a string of babbling words that sounded like a foreign language.

At that moment, Grace knew what had happened to June. She too had been given the gift of tongues.

But it was more than that. What Grace didn't know then was that this was just the beginning. Soon she would be touching the foreheads of thousands of people who would inexplicably crumble on the floor, some speaking in tongues, others healing miraculously, still others waking with intense spiritual refreshment.

Grace dumped the ice cubes into the sink. She looked toward the kitchen door that led out to the patio. Her neighbor Virginia had come back for her handbag. Stunned at seeing June on the linoleum floor speaking an eerie language, she grabbed her handbag from the kitchen table without saying a word and bolted out the door.

One afternoon a week later, Grace was in her kitchen breading eggplant and dropping cheese ravioli into boiling water. The family was having an early dinner. Larry was taking Larry, Junior, at six o'clock for a Little League game at Memorial Park. The twins, Christopher, and Grace would leave the house within the hour for the seven-thirty concert at St. Mary's in Ridgefield.

While Grace prepared the main course, Christopher, who was an eleven-year-old James Beard, made his special vinaigrette dressing for the tomato salad. As he did so, he supervised his mother. "Mom, you cut the eggplant all uneven!" Christopher held up two of the slices to prove his point. "And don't just dump all the raviolis into the pot at one time," he said sternly. "They'll get all yucky!"

There was no doubt in Grace's mind that one day her son would be a chef in his own snooty four-star restaurant. And there was no doubt in Christopher's mind that his mother would have to get her culinary act together if she ever wanted a job in his restaurant.

During dinner, the phone rang constantly, which was not unusual before a concert. The two guitarists called within minutes of each other to remind Grace to get to St. Mary's extra early for a quick run-through. The family knew why they were calling: The backup musicians wanted to make sure that Grace got there before the audience did. Punctuality was not high on Grace's list of priorities. She didn't believe in clocks.

At one point her family, who doubled as human alarm clocks, bought Grace a watch that they thought she would really like and wear. Grace loved the present. But she rarely looked at it and didn't even realize that it had stopped running until several weeks later when, out shopping, the watch read four o'clock. Grace felt that this must be wrong because she had just dropped the kids off at school. She stopped in at a jewelry and watch repair store at the shopping mall. A kindly faced gentleman wanted to know what the problem was. Grace told him that she had only had the watch a month and it had just stopped working. The man examined it. Then he wound it. "Oh," Grace blurted out, "I forgot you have to wind those things!"

A half-dozen other people called. Most wanted to know if Grace would save them extra seats. Twice Grace's mother phoned; the first time she asked what the twins wanted for their birthday, and five minutes later she called back to ask if they were too old for dolls.

"No, Mom. That's a great idea," Grace said into the phone. She was clearing the table at the same time. "You make wonderful dolls."

Grace just assumed that her mother would be making the girls their birthday present. Over the years, she had made everything from pillows to flowered sun hats to decorative dresser lamps. Her handicrafts were so delicately made that it was hard to believe that their maker was blind.

Antoinette was also only months away from receiving a degree from Westchester Community College. After graduation, she would work for the Women's Home League, a mental health association. She had been hired as a counselor for the mentally disturbed.

"I'm not making dolls this time!" Antoinette said in a tone that was half-scolding and half-incredulous. "What do you think, I've got nothing better to do than sit around stuffing dolls?" Antoinette reminded Grace that she was in the middle of final exams. This past semester she even had to drop out of the Light House Theater Company because of the heavy workload.

The Little League game that night was rained out in the third inning, but Grace, in St. Mary's auditorium, was unaware that a thunderstorm was going on. Over five hundred people clapping to the music screened out the sounds of the turbulent weather. It would have taken about a ten on the Richter scale to distract Grace when she was singing to God. It was as if she had entered another world. She felt she could almost reach up and touch Jesus.

That feeling of Jesus's presence had intensified in the last two weeks. Her experience of speaking in tongues was overpowering. Hearing God's voice say, "Go to my people. They do not know me," was equally overpowering.

This was all so profound that it left Grace feeling as if she were going to explode with God's love. Inside, she felt as if all her senses had been infinitely sharpened. Her vision had always been 20/20, but now it seemed to take on a new power. Several times recently she had come across individuals and, without ever having seen them before, she immediately knew things about them that she had no ordinary way of knowing. Two of the people were suicidal. The instant Grace set eyes on them, she knew they needed help.

Another was suffering from stomach cancer. The moment Grace made eye contact, she saw the person's disease and the need for help. But she did not know how to go about offering that help. She couldn't just stop strangers in a grocery store and start telling them about God and how fulfilled they would be with Jesus in their hearts.

Grace's hearing, too, was heightened. When she saw people whom she knew needed help, she heard an inner voice telling her that she should speak to them about God. The voice had no sound, yet it was strong and clear in her mind.

Many times over the past two weeks, Grace had gone into a quiet room in the house, fallen to her knees, and prayed for guidance. "Lord, I want to serve you," she would implore. "But I don't know how to go about it. I will do anything you desire. But show me, dear Lord. Help me. Guide me."

Now, inside St. Mary's, Grace's energy mounted. With each new song, the audience alternated between a breathless hush of expectation and infectious clapping and singing. The first two rows were taken up by a group of nuns who, during the upbeat gospel numbers, raised their arms, clapped their hands, and tapped their feet, looking for all the world as if they were at a Rolling Stones concert. By the third song, Grace had descended from the platform and joined the audience. With her jet-black hair and dark, flashing eyes, she was a striking figure in her turquoise gown. Her appearance commanded as much attention as her voice. But her sensitivity and sense of humor at times seemed to surpass both.

"Before I came here tonight," Grace began, "my son was on his way to a Little League game. As he kissed me good-bye, he asked if we could say a quick prayer to clobber the other team. I told him that we wouldn't say one prayer, but two—one for his team and one for the other team, to really give them something to sweat over.

"But you know," Grace added, for the first time acknowledging that there was a thunderstorm going on, "God clobbered both the teams!"

As a ripple of laughter died down, Grace's eyes scanned the audience. They focused on a man in a wheelchair in the middle aisle toward the rear of the auditorium. He looked to be in his mid-twenties. His face was blank. He appeared to be in pain and helpless. Suddenly Grace could see his anguish and suffering. She sensed that he had been left paralyzed from an accident. As her eyelids dropped, she saw a vision of him completely healed. She saw him leaving the wheelchair. Almost without her own volition, she began walking toward him.

As she approached his wheelchair, she heard the inner voice commanding her to tell him to be healed in the name of Jesus. Jesus's presence was strong, and this time Grace did not question the inner voice. The only thing that mattered was to follow it. She no longer felt foolish or self-conscious or that she was supposed to sing, not heal. At that moment, the five hundred people in the hall did not exist.

Grace placed her hand on top of the man's head. "Be healed in the name of Jesus."

The auditorium grew so quiet, you could hear the air conditioner go on and off.

"I want you to get up and walk!" Grace said, backing away from him.

The man's expression changed from a blank look to puzzlement. "I can't," he said. "I'm paralyzed. I've got a broken brain stem."

"Jesus just healed you!" Grace reached out her hand to his. "Come."

For a few seconds, the man just looked up at Grace, unable to take in her words. Then he began to lift himself out of his wheelchair. Shakily, he got to his feet. The audience gasped as the man stood, clutching Grace's hand.

"I want you to walk toward me," Grace commanded. She dropped his hand and backed away.

The man hesitated. He wiped his brow and took a step. The audience rose out of their seats. Grace began singing "Jesus Christ is King." He took a second step, and then a third. In moments, he was walking with only a limp up the long aisle. Tears flowed as he tried to speak to Grace. The words wouldn't come. He shook his head and fell into Grace's arms, sobbing.

Finally the young man said into the microphone, "The doctor told me that I'd never walk again."

Before he had a chance to return to his seat, dozens in the audience began moving toward the stage. They wanted healings too. Acting on what she was convinced were divine instructions, Grace laid her hands on their foreheads, telling them to be healed in the name of Jesus. After receiving Grace's touch, people fell backward onto the floor, dropping like stacked cards.

The musicians quickly jumped off the stage and caught them.

By the end of the evening, twenty people claimed that they had experienced instantaneous healings. Many others reported that they had felt the power of Christ enter their bodies when Grace laid her hands on them. Grace's life would never be the same—ever again.

In the wake of the meeting, phone calls came around the clock. Word spread from Ridgefield up to Hartford and as far as the Midwest. Friends and relatives of those who attended the service, total strangers, called to ask if they could bring their sick loved ones for a healing. One woman phoned from Kansas begging Grace to fly out, all expenses paid, to lay hands on her invalid husband. Another woman appeared at Grace's front door one night at ten o'clock and persuaded Grace to get in her car with her and drive thirty miles south to Stamford, Connecticut, where her sister was dying of cancer.

On a lighter note, Grace's two boys came home one afternoon with two of their friends and a sick hamster. Grace took one look at the tiny white rodent lying pathetically in a shoebox, let out a scream, and bolted the door shut.

News of Grace even spread to Larry's office at General Electric, where he was a computer systems analyst and project manager. While having lunch in the cafeteria one day, he overheard several secretaries discussing a woman called Grace who touched people and healed them. When one of the secretaries noticed Larry's curiosity, she asked if he would ever go to see the healer. Larry smiled and said, "Every night." He didn't reveal that she was his wife.

But not everyone was willing to accept what had happened at St. Mary's. And not everyone was healed.

Some who had been in the audience later accused Grace of planting the paralyzed man in the wheelchair. Some said that she had turned a sacred evening of gospel singing into a blasphemous sideshow. Some claimed that it was an act of the devil, and that she should be banned from ever singing again on Catholic grounds.

These accusations came in letters and over the telephone. Some gave their names; others were anonymous. But the sharpest attack took place two weeks afterward at another prayer meeting at St. Mary's. Grace attended the meeting fully aware that some of the people who had phoned and written letters of protest would be there. But she also felt that she had no choice but to show up. Not to go would be an admission that she had done something sacrilegious. And Grace believed more strongly than ever that she had followed God's divine will.

She arrived a few minutes late. She wanted to make sure that she didn't have to stand around feeling uncomfortable. With a good deal of reluctance, she walked into the auditorium and scanned the large room for someone whom she knew was on her side. Everyone was already seated. There were only a few empty seats in the last row. Hesitantly, Grace sat down next to a woman who had written one of the letters. The woman looked straight ahead, not acknowledging that anyone had sat down beside her. Feeling the cold shoulder, Grace hoped that at any moment the prayers would begin. The power of prayer, she was sure, would override the hostility that seemed to be coming from every direction.

There was no subtlety about what followed. The topic of the discussion was "Healers and How to Test the Spirit for Legitimacy." When Grace heard that, it

took all of her courage to remain seated. But not everyone in the group felt Grace had acted in a blasphemous
way. Some who had been at the gospel concert stood
and gave testimony that Grace had healed them by the
laying on of hands. One woman said that a lump in
her neck had instantly dissolved. Another claimed that
for the first time in five years she had been able to go
off sleeping pills. Still another said that she had been
freed from crippling arthritis. And she did a little dance
with her fingers to demonstrate to the group how nimble they had become.

Then, however, a self-appointed leader representing
the other side stood, and although she addressed herself
to the entire group, she seemd to focus her eyes only
on Grace.

"As I said earlier, I think that it is of utmost importance that we make *sure* that any 'purported healing' is of God—and not the devil."

Grace did not stand to defend herself. She dropped
her head. The woman continued to speak about hysterical healings and emotionalism.

"Dear God," Grace said silently in prayer, "I didn't
do anything. You did it. I don't understand how this
could all be happening." Tears welled in her eyes while
others stood up to speak.

"I'm in complete agreement," a man whom Grace
recognized as one of the church ushers said. "One must
be on the lookout for individuals claiming the gift of
healing as a self-serving motive."

Another man stood up and added, "Especially if that
'individual' is already in the entertainment business."

This was clearly a witch hunt. Grace had had enough.
She gathered her sweater and handbag and was just
about to step out into the aisle to leave when she sud-

denly felt as if someone were physically holding her down. But nobody was touching her. Stunned, she sat back. Then she heard the inner voice of God say, "I will defend you."

A woman from one of the front rows stood. It was Sister Martha, a Notre Dame nun and one of the most erudite and respected members of the Catholic community. Grace steeled herself for what Sister Martha was about to say. It was one thing, Grace thought, for one of the ushers to stand and accuse her of blasphemy. But if Sister Martha did too, it would be more than she could handle.

"Excuse me," the nun began, "but I have no doubt that that *was* the power of the Holy Spirit of God using this woman. I believe that Jesus is alive. And that He is working through Grace. We often pray. Right here we pray." She extended her arm and pointed around the room. "We pray that God will do these kinds of things. But when God uses someone in our midst, we then want to dictate to God. We want to tell Him that He can't use her. She's not educated enough in theology. But I feel that God did choose her.

"I was here that night. And I had a healing too." There was complete silence as Sister Martha told how Grace had placed her hand on her shoulder, taking all the pain from her bursitis away.

Although Sister Martha's seal of approval did not cap the controversy, it did end the letters, phone calls, and verbal abuse—temporarily, anyway. Later, when one of the parishioners questioned the pastor about Grace's healing, he was heard to say, "If Grace has Sister Martha behind her, who or what could be against her?" He spoke whimsically, but there was an element of truth to those words.

Perhaps the controversy itself spread the word about Grace to the various churches throughout the area, for within a month of that first healing, she had been invited to a half-dozen churches of various denominations. And by the end of the first year, she had performed healing services in over a hundred churches and auditoriums in southern Connecticut.

Local newspaper reporters became regulars at her doorstep. Sometimes their stories were handled in a serious vein. Sometimes they were slanted to be tongue-in-cheek. Usually, however, they were somewhere in the middle. But always the headlines were bold and dramatic: WORKING MIRACLES . . . THEY CALL HER AMAZING . . . TRAVELING EVANGELIST AND HER BAND MAKE CLAIMS OF MIRACLE CURES . . . FAITH HEALER CURES THOUSANDS BY SINGING TO THEM . . . THEY SEEK THE TOUCH OF GRACE.

The accompanying photographs added to the drama—pictures of people falling backward, lying all over the floor as if there had been a bloodless battle, and pictures of people with their hands raised, eyes closed, and lips moving in prayer. If these pictures had appeared anywhere but in the staid Northeast, Grace might not have been received by such an incredulous audience. People in this part of the country generally tended to lump "healers" into the same category as snake oil and moon dust.

However, one particular feature drew a good deal of positive attention in the Catholic community. It was a two-part article in *The Greenwich Times*, a newspaper that serves one of the most affluent towns in the country, if not the world. The headline on the front page read, THE SINGING EVANGELIST: SHE PRAYS TO HEAL THE SICK. Below the headline were five photos. One of those depicted Grace kneeling over a man who was lying flat on his back. Standing next to Grace was a monsignor holding a bottle of anointing oil. The caption read, "Healing Prayers: Mrs. DiBicarri and Monsignor James J. McLaughlin pray with others that Ronald Cherico's crippled legs be straightened." In the article, Bridget McTigue, the staff reporter, wrote:

It seemed an unlikely beginning for the event that was to follow. A Saturday night healing service with gospel-rock music in a Roman Catholic church in Greenwich.

Monsignor James J. McLaughlin, a graying priest clothed in a black cassock with red piping, stepped out onto the altar of St. Agnes Church, its pews filled with more than 300 people.

"I don't think I'm the Charismatic type," he began as the crowd listened attentively. McLaughlin was referring to the Charismatic Renewal, a spiritual revival movement within the Catholic Church that fosters a personal, "Born Again" relationship with Christ through the Holy Spirit. "But I'm deeply impressed by what the Charismatics have to offer," he continued.

"It's all scripture-oriented, and I like that. This interest they have in the Word of God is basic to our faith. And Charismatics pray a lot. I like that, too. God told us to pray always, lest we fall into temptation. Charismatics are a happy people. This drew me to them."

With that, he left the altar of the crowded Stanwich Road church, and the gospel-rock band, "Grace 'N Vessels of Christ," began to play.

The second of the two-part feature ran the very next day. Again on the front page, the bold print read, THEY TELL OF HAVING BEEN HEALED. The same journalist wrote:

A Hollywood film studio executive and his wife, who had attended one of Mrs. DiBicarri's services, flew her [Grace] to Cleveland to pray for the 20-year-old son of a well-known politician. The boy, away at college, had fallen and struck his head on a table. A large blood clot had formed in his brain and he slipped into a coma. The clot was surgically removed, but the boy remained comatose.

The young man's family finally summoned Mrs. DiBicarri as a last resort, three and a half weeks later. The night she arrived at the hospital, she sang Christian songs and prayed over the youth. According to the film executive's wife in a phone interview from Beverly Hills, the young man emerged from his coma and reached out his hand to his father.

Mrs. DiBicarri remained at the hospital, praying daily, for one week. By the end of the week, the young man recognized members of his family and some of his belongings, and was able to utter sounds.

From there, he progressed to sitting in a wheelchair, reading, writing and talking. Now, several months later, the youth's father says his son is able to walk with the aid of a walker. The family and Mrs. DiBicarri are still praying for a total healing.

Grace returned from Cleveland to her house, which looked as if it had been ripped by a tornado. "Sorry about the slightly messy house, Mom," Karen said. She handed her mother three shoeboxes filled with letters, along with a stack of phone messages.

"Some of the people who called," Karen said, picking up empty soda bottles and potato chip wrappers from the coffee tables, "were so upset that me, Sharon, Christopher, and Larry began praying with them over the phone. Hope that was okay?"

"It's not okay, it's fantastic!" Grace said. "You won't believe this but on the plane ride home, I suddenly got an idea. Since all these people are calling for help—and since it would be impossible for me to go all over the country to do individual healings—I thought we might start up a telephone prayer line. You know," Grace added, "a twenty-four-hour one."

"Yeah," Sharon said, "for all those who need help right away!"

Grace went on to explain that the only thing that concerned her was how she could carry on the prayer line all by herself. She told the kids that she didn't want to force this on them.

"Mom," Larry, who was sixteen, said. "I talked to a man for an hour the other night. He was real sad. And we prayed together. And before he got off the phone, he said that he felt real good. Like I was his grandson or something. I hope he calls back when I'm on duty."

By the time they went to bed that night, the decision was unanimous: The prayer line would go in. And each teenager would have a specific time for phone duty. They even drew up a preliminary time schedule. But they could always swap hours; the rules, Grace stressed, could be relaxed. "I don't want any of you to feel obligated," Grace said, "but I must warn you that the first time someone isn't home during his hours, it's either the death penalty or cleaning up your room. And I don't want you choosing the former as a cop-out."

A week later, when a man from the phone company arrived, Grace led him down the stairs and into the basement.

"My office is right over there," she said, pointing to a door. Then she ran back upstairs, where someone was waiting on the phone. A few minutes later the confused telephone man came upstairs. He told Grace that he couldn't seem to find her office. "The only thing that's down there is a little closet with a boiler in it," he said.

"That's right," Grace said cheerfully. "As soon as my husband takes the boiler out, I'll move a desk in and set up my office."

The man raised his eyebrows and darted his eyes around the room as if someone were going to come out and say, "Smile, you're on Candid Camera."

CHAPTER SIX ⚜⚜

GRACE'S HEADQUARTERS REMAINED IN THE boiler-room office for the next three years. During that time, she performed healing services in churches around her hometown. By the second year, her reputation had spread to the lay community. She was now being invited to give services in convalescent homes, prisons, and at the Danbury Fair.

Because so much of Grace's time was spent away from home, especially on weekends, the official family policy adopted was that, whenever possible, everyone would attend Grace's services. The family loved to sit in the audience, singing and praying along with Grace. Sometimes they would help seat people.

Christopher, Grace's younger son, was active in her ministry. At fifteen, he had a passion not only for cooking but also for the drums. His mother did not let his budding talent go unrecognized. She made him a backup musician, along with guitarists Ron Borakto and David Fields.

Grace often thought of the healing services as icing

on the cake. They were jubilant and rewarding; when Grace was singing to God, she felt as if she were no longer part of this world—as if she were suspended halfway between earth and heaven. On the other hand, some of the phone calls that came in over the twenty-four-hour prayer line brought her back to the cold fact that life on earth isn't easy.

Within months of the prayer line being installed, phone calls were coming in around the clock. It was not unusual for Grace or one of the volunteers to be on the phone half the night with someone on the verge of suicide. If that person lived nearby, volunteers David Fields, Denise Dostie, Ron Borakto, or Grace herself would drive to the person's home and continue to pray with him or her. But the majority of callers asked for physical and financial miracles.

"People weren't calling because they wanted prayer for zillions of dollars," Grace recalled. "They simply wanted enough money to put food on the table for their families. Jesus says that faith without works is dead. It isn't enough just to pray. You have to do everything in your power to make things better. And in these cases, it meant getting food to the hungry.

"I remember one of the first homes I brought food to, less than three miles from where we lived. It was for a woman with no husband, three small children, and one on the way. The place was a shambles. The woman was in bed with dangerously high blood pressure. The kids were running around half dressed. The mother kept apologizing for the condition of the house. She said that her doctor warned if she got out of bed she could lose the baby, and maybe her own life too. The woman had no money for help to take care of her children. While I was in the bedroom praying with her,

80

the children were devouring the food. It had been their first meal in two days.

"As I drove home, I began to cry," Grace continued. "I told Jesus that He would have to give me a lot more strength if I was supposed to see hungry children. I thought about my own childhood. As poor as we were, we always had food on the table. I never realized that right in my own town there were people starving. It was a real awakening. And frankly, I didn't know if I was cut out for it.

"I went to bed and prayed again. I asked God if He could give just one sign that He would provide me the strength to cope with one of the worst realities of life, hunger. I guess it was about two in the morning when I suddenly awakened. It was as if someone had turned a thousand-watt light bulb on in my head. In that instant, all my fears lifted. I was filled with confidence.

"As I was thanking God for the sudden courage, an entire plan of action flashed before me, as if on a mental motion picture screen. He was showing me that I was supposed to organize the women in our neighborhood to form a meals-on-wheels type of program. Each day, a different woman would be assigned to prepare and deliver meals to a specified home.

"The very next day I had eight volunteers. By the end of the first year, there were twenty-six women making it possible for every person who needed food to receive regular daily meals."

Also by the second year in the boiler room office, the number of letters Grace received had grown to several hundred. Most were from people who wanted to let her know of a healing they had received and/or how God had come into their lives, filling a void.

Grace's filing system for these letters was not based

on any Harvard Business School text. All incoming letters went into a file box made out of an A&P grocery carton. The outgoing mail went into a metal coal bucket painted a bright red, which Sharon had picked up for twenty-five cents at a school rummage sale. At the end of each week, Grace took the red coal bucket with all the letters, which she had personally answered in longhand, to the post office. The postage cost ran close to a hundred dollars a month. Since Grace had not yet begun to collect donations at the services, all the office expenses—flyers heralding the next service, toll calls, and postage—came out of the household budget. Fortunately, Larry was earning enough as a systems analyst that the family didn't have to skimp on groceries for their four fast-growing teenagers.

At the end of the third year, the boiler room could barely hold another paper clip. Grace decided that it was time to move to a real office where they would have space to assemble the monthly flyer, sort mail, schedule services, develop photographs, and perform other office duties that had escalated in the four years.

After weeks of scouring the Danbury-Brookfield area, David Fields found an ad in the paper that read, "Modern ranch house. Commercially zoned. Easily converted into office space." An hour later, Grace and David pulled into the driveway of the Brookfield house. As the landlord gave them a tour of the very ordinary ranch house, Grace suddenly felt that this was the right place for her ministry. Standing in the empty living room, she envisioned a chapel. Above the fireplace, she saw the large framed painting of Jesus that now hung in her playroom. Instead of a sofa, end tables, and wingbacks, she saw metal folding chairs for Bible study classes. The bedroom would serve as an office. All the closet and pantry space would be used for supplies.

Without even asking what the rent was, Grace said that she would take it. But moments later, upon learning that it was $550 per month, she had to explain that that was way out of her league. She would have to look elsewhere. The landlord, discovering what the property would be used for, asked her how much she *could* afford.

"Maybe three hundred dollars?" Grace said tentatively. She was afraid that he would say no. And she was even more afraid that if he did say yes, she still couldn't afford it.

There was no haggling. The man simply said, "Fine. You promise to keep it clean and well maintained, and it's yours."

He even waived the security deposit on good faith and gave her an extra thirty days to raise the first month's rent. The deal was sealed with a flyer about her next service and twelve dollars, plus some odd change that she dug out of her purse, for a down payment.

On May 1, 1981, one week after the lease had been signed, Grace, David, and her two sons moved a maple desk, dozens of cartons stuffed with three years' worth of letters and papers, and everything else out of the boiler room and into a pick-up truck. Then, with Christopher riding in the back to make sure that the cartons didn't overturn, they drove the two miles to the new office in Brookfield. The entire move was accomplished in three trips. It could have taken only one, but Grace kept thinking of furniture in her home that she could borrow so that the ministry's headquarters wouldn't look so empty.

Only one thing cast a shadow on the excitement of moving: Grace would have to begin to ask for donations at the services. This was something she did not look forward to. But the facts were plain: If the ministry didn't take in five hundred dollars every month to meet the overhead—rent, utilities, and phone—it would be back to the boiler room. A cardboard box sat on a card table at every service. It was marked LOVE OFFERING.

The first month, less than two hundred dollars were collected from the box. Fortunately, the landlord had given Grace an additional month before she had to begin paying the rent. During this time, Grace prayed for God's help, and more specifically for someone who could run the entire ministry.

At the beginning of the second month, she was convinced that her prayers had been answered: Larry James, who is now Grace's guitarist and executive vice-president of the ministry, first phoned then. But he didn't phone about a job. He called for help for the deep anxiety that made him unable to function. The symptoms had been debilitating: There was constant trembling in his hands. His eyes twitched. He had frequent migraines. He was so filled with fear that he could not leave his house, sometimes for weeks at a time. Thinking that he had some dread disease, Larry went from doctor to doctor in search of a cure. The only relief he was ever offered was heavy tranquilizers. Larry had seen many of his friends end up wasted on drugs. He refused to believe that drugs, even if prescribed by a doctor, were the answer. But he didn't know what his answer was.

Larry had come from Middletown, Connecticut, where he had hosted a successful syndicated radio show, plus a weekly musical TV program. In his mid-twenties, after several years of local success, Larry decided that it was time to break into the big time. He packed up his personal belongings, said good-bye to his family and friends, and left for California.

Six weeks later, he returned. Life in Hollywood was not what he had imagined it would be. Everyone who had even a moderate amount of success seemed to be on drugs. This was clearly not how he wanted to end up. Larry had given his life to Jesus when he was sixteen. His brother's girlfriend had left a Bible in the house, which he had picked up, and suddenly he found himself reading it right straight through. When he finished, he was convinced that it was the word of God.

Nearly a year after Larry returned from California and six months after his anxiety symptoms first manifested, his mother showed him an article about Grace in the newspaper. She asked Larry if he thought there was anything to it. Larry did believe that some people had the gift of healing, but he didn't know if this woman did.

It took him several phone calls to locate Grace. Finally he was successful. The following week, he attended a service only miles from where he lived. As Larry sat in the audience listening to Grace sing and watching the laying on of hands, an anxiety attack forced him to leave halfway through the service. He hadn't even had a chance to receive a healing.

The next day, unable to shake the service from his mind, he called the prayer-line number to ask for help. Grace answered.

"I've got this nervous problem," he told her. "There's all these symptoms. About a hundred of them."

But Grace didn't seem to be interested in Larry's nervous condition. Instead she asked, "You don't play the guitar, do you?"

Larry was taken aback. He hadn't mentioned anything about music. He suddenly wondered if she thought he was somebody else. He reintroduced himself and said that he was phoning for special prayer. He was really sick and needed help.

"Do you sing too?" was Grace's next question.

"You don't understand," Larry said. "I'm a nervous wreck."

Grace was relentless. "Have you ever done any TV?"

The conversation went on like this, with Larry practically begging for prayer for his condition and Grace ignoring his pleas. Finally Larry said, "Excuse me, Grace, but I'm in no position to sing, play a guitar, or do anything else. My hands are shaking so badly right now that I can barely hold this telephone."

"We're going to pray right now," Grace said. "Together. Over the phone."

And together they prayed. But Grace was not praying for Larry's acute anxiety to go away. She was praying for him to work with her in the ministry.

Two weeks later, Larry had an office at the ministry's headquarters. Five days after that, he was lead guitarist for the healing services. And several months after that, he purchased video equipment, to put the healing services on cable TV. A year later, Grace would be seen each week by an estimated ten million viewers around the country. Acute anxiety and all its symptoms were now only a memory for Larry.

As the ministry grew, the number of volunteer helpers grew with it. It was not difficult to discern why. Grace was having remarkable success helping deeply troubled persons—those with hopeless drug and alcohol addictions, those with deep-rooted psychological and emotional problems, and those who were on the verge of suicide.

It was most startling to those addicted that they were

86

able to break instantly from their habits—and experience no withdrawal symptoms whatever. And those with emotional problems were able to function again very suddenly.

The former addicts were the people, particularly, who unstintingly offered their services to Grace's ministry. Perhaps half of the dozen on her volunteer staff were in this category. In fact, three of the male ushers, Carmine, Al, and Jerry, at one time strangers, now shared a common camaraderie: All had been delivered from drugs and alcohol. All had turned their lives over to God and had become productive human beings. During her services, Grace sometimes asks one of them to come forward and tell his story so that others can be helped. Al's testimony is especially moving. He is the youngest and came the closest to not making it.

"I met Grace over two years ago. I was twenty-three," Al told the audience at a Greenwich High School service. "I was taking cocaine, LSD, alcohol. I didn't care what it was, as long as I got wiped out—wasted. When I wasn't drunk or stoned, the only thoughts I had were of suicide. I was empty inside, searching for something. But I didn't think I'd ever find whatever it was I was looking for.

"The day I planned on ending it all, I had seen a poster in a small shop in Waterbury announcing one of Grace's services. I didn't even know why my eye caught it. I had been in that shop a thousand times before and never saw that poster before. It said something about 'Do you need a miracle in your life?' I didn't believe it. In fact, I don't even know what made me ever go to that service. But I was desperate.

"I remember sitting way in the back of the auditorium. I said to myself, 'God if you're real, show me.'

"Grace was talking about coming forward and inviting God into your life," Al recalled. "Every word she said seemed to be for me. Let me play you the tape of that service I brought." He snapped on a small cassette recorder that he carried with him. Grace's voice was scratchy, but I could understand the words.

"Deep within you, you are suffering," Grace was telling the five hundred people in the audience. "Perhaps long ago, someone said something. Somebody did something. It hurt you. You held in that hurt. Since that time, you've thought about it now and again. When it comes to mind, the hurt rises up within you. As a result, you've developed a deep bitterness toward the one who hurt you. The pain often drives you into a depressive state. Given time, that sickness inside your mind will blossom into sickness of your body.

"Most don't even know how deep or far advanced the sickness inside them has grown. It works like a time bomb. A painful situation occurs. Emotions are planted deep inside. Once there, they grow into resentment, bitterness, guilt, fear, hate, and self-pity. They begin to take over your mind. To ease the pain, you take drugs, alcohol.

"But this destructive cycle can be broken through a divine healing," Grace said. "When the Lord heals from within, the healing is as wonderful and complete as when He heals the outer body. Jealousy will be replaced with trust; resentment with acceptance; bitterness with forgiveness; anger with peace; self-pity with security; and hatred with love.

"But maybe you're sitting there saying, 'But, Grace, you don't understand. I have deep hurts from my childhood. They've been with me all my life. I'll always have those scars.' All right, maybe you do have deep

88

hurts. Perhaps you've had them all your life. If you keep concentrating on those feelings, you will always have them. But if you choose to look to Jesus, He'll remove them. *He* is the healer. *He* wants to be your healer and make you whole. Will you let Him?''

Al snapped off the recorder abruptly. Then he said, ''I don't know what suddenly happened to me. Something just lifted me off my chair. I was the first person to walk down to the front of the stage area. Then there were a whole lot of others around me. But Grace pointed to me and said, 'You've been very depressed. It takes guts to come up here.'

''I fell back. She was about twenty feet from me. About five minutes later, I came to. I got up and I felt joyful. I had also been smoking about three packs of cigarettes a day. After the service, I got in my car and lit up. But it tasted awful and I threw it out. That was the last cigarette I had. After that night, I had no desire for a drink or a drug.''

A year later Al married Donna, the secretary at the ministry. And a year after that, they opened up two stores at a mall in Waterbury.

This was Al's testimony, but it could be the testimony of many of Grace's other volunteer staffers. During the months I spent with Grace, I became close to these men and women, known as ''the Vessels.'' At first I didn't quite know what to make of Carmine, who wears a gold earring in one ear and said ''Praise God'' at the end of every question I asked him. But I soon learned that he is as sincere as the others.

The ushers—especially the ''catchers'' who perform the critical function of breaking the fall of those who ''fall out in the Spirit''—play an important role at the services. Just how important was dramatized one evening in front of several skeptical people whom I had persuaded to attend a service with me. They included social commentator Vance Packard and his artist wife, Virginia; Dr. David Goodrich, a psychologist, and his wife, Eleanor, a chemical engineer; Dr. Paul Schulman, a cancer specialist, and his wife, Susan, an anthropologist; and their friend Lars-Eric Lindblad, an explorer and naturalist.

We were all in the front row. When Grace called forward those who wanted to accept the Lord as their personal savior, a crowd of eight deep formed at the apron of the stage. After Grace had led the group in prayer, she began to call out the names of various afflictions. The healings occur during this part of the service. One woman, about twenty feet away from Grace but only inches from Dr. Schulman, began to waver when Grace pointed to her and said, "That pain down the right side of your neck is to be lifted. Now!"

I had warned everyone except the Schulmans what to expect. I had planned to give them a brief rundown before the service, but they arrived late. The only thing they were expecting to see was a gospel concert with Grace praying for people to be healed.

The moment I saw where the woman Grace had pointed to was standing, I realized that there was no time to explain to the Schulmans that some people fall over backward when Grace lays hands on them or points to them from a distance. It was happening at that very moment. There were no catchers in the vicinity. I only had time to turn to Paul, six seats away, and yell, "Grab her!"

Stunned, he threw out his arms and caught the middle-aged woman in her proper navy blue suit with her handbag draped over her shoulder.

Susan Schulman let out a slight gasp as she helped her husband lower the woman to the auditorium floor. Neither of them had any idea that this was all part of what usually happens. Concerned, Paul leaned over the woman, and just as he began to open her eyes to check life signs, people shouted from all directions, "Leave her alone!"

"Don't touch her!" screeched two elderly women sitting behind him.

"I'm a medical doctor!" Paul said, turning to those around him.

At that point, two of the ushers came toward him and gently pulled the bewildered doctor from the lady, who was out cold on the floor. "God's working on her," they told him.

More confused than ever, Paul brought his hand up to his chin and sat down again.

Later in the service, David Goodrich and his wife decided to see what it was like to receive a healing. They joined the crowd at the stage. Grace approached Eleanor first. Placing her thumb lightly to the petite engineer's ear, Grace whispered something to her. Moments later, Eleanor reeled back in a stiff-legged stagger. An usher gently eased her down to the auditorium floor. David, shocked to see that his wife had passed out cold, let out a yelp. "That's my wife!" he told Grace, who was now standing in front of him.

"She's fine," Grace quietly consoled. Then she placed one hand over David's heart and another to his forehead. "Jesus, heal this man's heart condition!"

The doctor jerked his head away. "How did you know there's anything wrong with my heart?" he asked.

"It's the word of God," Grace said in the tone and manner of a physician who has just read an angiogram result. Her palm was pressed to the middle of his chest. Her eyes were closed tightly. She appeared to be in deep prayer. David, however, was obviously more concerned about his wife, who was still lying on the high school floor, than he was about receiving a healing, and he kept turning to look anxiously at her. Grace remained praying over him for a few minutes more before she moved on to the next person in the healing line.

Before David went back to his seat, he knelt down beside his wife. "Eleanor," he said, giving her arm a slight shove, "you okay?"

One of the ushers came right over and asked him to take his seat. "God's not quite done with her yet."

David, as confused as Paul Schulman had been by that answer, returned to his seat, but he still kept a close eye on his wife. Five minutes later, she got up, brushed off her skirt, and sat down next to her husband. His face showed immense relief as she smiled at him.

It was several days before I was able to follow up on what had happened that night and to get the further reactions of these two professional couples, who had experienced such culture shock at the service. I first talked to Eleanor Goodrich.

"You know, Liz," Eleanor said during our phone conversation, "in spite of all the singing and hand clapping, it was a very peaceful experience. When Grace touched my forehead, I felt a calmness come over me."

"Did you expect that?" I asked.

"Not at all. But when it happened, I didn't fight it."

"And that's when you went over backward?"

"Exactly," she said. "It was as if I temporarily lost consciousness. I lay there, and the only thing I was aware of was the music playing in the background."

As Eleanor was talking about how relaxing and

peaceful she had felt, semiconscious on the auditorium floor, David got on the extension. "Something's definitely going on there," he said.

"David, did you feel anything when she laid hands on you?" I asked.

"Well, I'll tell you," he said, "I was so distracted to see Eleanor on the floor that I don't really recall what I felt." Then he added quizzically, "Did you mention anything about my heart problem to Grace?"

I reminded David that I didn't even know that he had a heart problem. And even if I had known, I said, I made it a rule never to mention to Grace anything personal about the people I bring. But it was true that every time Grace diagnosed any of my friends' conditions, they automatically assumed that I had given her their personal medical history.

Virginia Packard had certainly thought so. When she went up for a healing, Grace placed her hand over Virginia's lower spine and said, "This lower back pain is to go!"

Virginia returned to her seat convinced that I had told Grace that she had lower back pain. I had to convince her that I wasn't even aware that she had had a problem with her back.

"Did the back pain go?" David asked.

"Well, this is what is so strange," I said. "The next morning when I called Virginia, she said that the back pain was still there, but a bothersome skipped heartbeat wasn't."

"What did Vance Packard say about that?" David asked.

"He just said he was totally baffled."

"All I can say," David said, "is that I'm totally baffled too."

"That makes three of us," I said. "I've been researching Grace's story for ten months. I've been to over forty services, interviewed several hundred people who claim healings, and have gathered medical documentation on dozens, and I'm still no closer to a nonreligious explanation than when I first started out."

"Do you interview these people on the spot?" Eleanor wanted to know.

"If I'm there at the time," I said. "Otherwise I get their names and telephone numbers through the ministry's office."

"Are any of these people reticent about discussing their healings with you?" David asked.

"No, not at all." I told him about a woman I had talked to in her car in the parking lot after the service. I had noticed her going in, supported by two others, unable to walk at all. Afterward, she told me it was her first service. She hadn't wanted to go, but her daughter had insisted. When she got into the healing line, Grace placed her hands over her legs, which were crippled with arthritis. She said that the pain instantly lifted. She still needed help getting back to her seat, but when they got up to leave, she felt a tingling sensation run from her hips to her toes. "Something is happening to my legs," she said to her daughter. Then she walked out into the aisle without help.

I asked the woman how she felt now. Instead of telling me, she showed me. She flung the car door open, got out, and ran around the parking lot, half shouting and half crying, "I can't believe it! Thank you, Jesus!"

"Well, what happened to me is certainly not as dramatic as what happened to that woman," Eleanor then said. "But it's really quite amazing.

"After the service when we got home, I felt a little hungry. I made myself a snack, a bowl of granola with milk. Halfway through eating the cereal, I suddenly realized that I had been chewing the coarse nuggets on the left side of my mouth. This was something I hadn't been able to do for months because of extreme tenderness in my gums.

"I had kept putting off going to the dentist for X-rays," Eleanor went on. "I was hoping that it would go away. But it seemed to get worse—until the other night. That's when it went away, and it hasn't come back."

Before we hung up, David said that he and Eleanor were planning to go to the next service.

The following Wednesday, I met with Susan Schulman. Although Susan had not experienced a physical healing as Eleanor had, she admitted that she had been equally impressed. She felt she had received a certain peace of mind from the evening.

"I came home Friday night," Susan said, "and I said to Paul, 'You know, death doesn't seem so terrible.' The whole phenomenon was amazing."

"What on earth did you think when you first arrived?" I asked.

"First of all, I must tell you that when we drove up and saw the mob, I got uncomfortable. Then when we found out that you had saved us seats in the front row, I panicked. Here we were sitting in such a prime place. I felt it wasn't right. We were intruders. We both felt plainly and simply uncomfortable."

"Because of the religion aspect?"

"Here we are Jewish," Susan said. "And on top of that, it's Passover. Not that we're religious, but still, everyone was clapping and praising Jesus. Everyone seemed so involved."

"Did that bother you?"

"I'll tell you what did bother me: when Grace started

to point to different people, calling out their diseases and bringing them up there. I realized then that I had to avoid eye contact. I felt that if I didn't have eye contact with her, she couldn't point to me and bring me up there."

"Did you think that she might?"

"Yes. And I didn't feel that my head or heart was in it."

"I saw the look on your faces when that lady tumbled into Paul's arms," I said.

"When I saw that happen, I panicked again," Susan said. "I totally panicked. I didn't expect it. But just before that, during Grace's singing, which is beautiful, I was clapping my hands. Paul and I kind of got into it a little bit. Then when that large group moved up close to the stage, I said to Paul, 'I'm not going to stand up. I don't want to be part of that large group.' Just as I said that, the woman fell over into Paul's arms. After I came out of shock, I became skeptical. I felt that it was all the power of the mind and the desire for hope."

"You mean that it seemed to be just an emotional trip?" I asked.

"I thought that at first," Susan replied. "But then I must tell you that after I saw the number of people who seemed genuinely touched, my skepticism began to wane. There were things that happened there that even Paul couldn't explain, and he's a physician."

"I noticed Paul go up to the usher holding the jar of anointing oil," I said. "Did he ask her something?"

"Oh, that," Susan said, as she gave a quick laugh. "Paul asked for a sample of the oil. He thought maybe it was ether."

"And?"

"It was just ordinary oil," Susan said. "But I'll tell you, her perfume was very, very strong. I thought maybe if you were close enough to her and you inhaled that, you'll go down."

"Except that doesn't explain why people go down twenty feet away, when Grace merely points to them. Like that first woman," I said.

"Well, that's all part of the mystery," Susan said. "I felt that the test would come with Lars. I said to Paul, 'Lars won't go down.' Lars is an intelligent, sophisticated, non-Godly person. I can relate to him. I said to Paul, 'He's not going to go down."

"Paul said, 'Of course he isn't.' And all of a sudden Lars was at my feet, flat on the floor. Oh my God, I said to myself. And then Lars gets up and walks over to us and says that it was the most incredible experience he had ever had."

"That's when Paul got into the healing line," I added.

"That's right," Susan said. "Paul wanted to give it a try too."

"Just because Lars went down?" I asked.

"Well, that, and probably because of all the others, and all those who said they were healed after Grace touched them. When Paul got into that line, I thought, if he goes down, I won't even be able to drive that car home!"

"But Paul didn't go down," I said.

"He worked at *not* going down," Susan said, "just the way I did. He said he smelled the very strong perfume, and he tried not to inhale it deeply. And he kept his mind unreceptive to it. I did the same thing. I stood in the line before Grace, and my mind was totally closed. I concentrated on one of the flowers on the stage. I just totally removed myself from the situation. I had almost fainted fifteen times before I got up there. In the course of the evening, I had gone from sweating to freezing. I had gone through a whole psychological change. To think that in the span of just three hours, I went from being totally uncomfortable to going up there waiting for the experience. Knowing me, that is a phenomenon unto itself."

"Were you afraid of falling over?"

"Yes, of losing control," Susan said. "But the next time, I'll be more comfortable." Then she added, "You know, it was joyful. At the end I *really* felt good. Afterward, we went out—we hadn't eaten dinner yet. And we talked for an hour and a half. And again in the morning, we described it to our kids explicitly. They were very intrigued."

"Do you have any doubts about the healings you saw?" I asked.

"Of course," Susan said. "But then again, just being married to Paul, I've seen over the years that people who have the will to live, actually do live longer."

"Did Paul feel as if she were alienating the medical community?"

"Not at all," Susan said. "It was quite the contrary."

"Because of what she said—about going back to your own doctors?"

"No, I don't think it was her statements. I think it was her manner. She was not saying, Eat apricot pits and you will be cured. She was approaching it from a totally different and unique perspective, as a religious person, not as a scientist. They are not mutually dependent approaches. They're mutually exclusive. Gosh, if I were dying, I would go for everything, wouldn't you? I could see the peace of mind you would get. I got it just from sitting there being totally healthy."

During the months I spent with Grace, I continually looked for parallel phenomena to help me accept what appeared to be miraculous. One particular item that struck me was an abstract in the prestigious *Journal of the American Medical Association.*

The item concerned the heavily documented case of a twenty-eight-year-old woman from the Philippines who had been diagnosed at several medical centers in Washington as having systemic lupus erythematosus, a serious immunological disease that affects the liver and lymphatic system. After she was treated with a hormone drug, other complications developed, including thyroid and kidney dysfunction. With each different drug she used, more complications arose.

After several months of unsuccessful treatments, the *Journal* reported that the woman had decided, against the advice of her physicians and family, to return to her native Philippine village to see the local faith healer. The day she left, medical tests again confirmed what the doctors already knew about her disease.

To the surprise of everyone except the woman herself, she returned in three weeks completely healed and has remained that way ever since. Two years later, she gave birth to a healthy child.

It wasn't long afterward that I came across a paper in *The American Theosophist* written by prominent psychiatrist George L. Hogben, who is on the teaching staff of the Mount Sinai Medical Center in Manhattan. His explanation of healings seemed to be more in line with Grace's.

"The spiritual nature of the individual is an essential part of the healing process," Hogben wrote. "Whether we know it or not, God is our healer, and God's Spirit is the energy for our healing. The various healing techniques we employ all act by channeling the energy of the Spirit on our behalf. The healing force of God's

Spirit transforms suffering and pain to love and compassion. The experience of God dwelling within provides enduring meaning to our lives."

Dr. Hogben felt it was critical that spirituality be brought into the healing process as soon as possible. "Even a faint glimpse of the beauty of the nonmaterial reality," he wrote, "can provide a person with the meaning necessary to continue a healing path."

Perhaps this could be one explanation of how the woman from the Philippines and those who attended Grace's services were healed. Perhaps they were elevated to the point where they glimpsed the nonmaterial world, as Hogben stated.

"In the final analysis, healing is the experience of the love and forgiveness from the working of God's Spirit," Hogben wrote. "Each time we give up pain and feel the love from God's Spirit rushing in to take its place, we learn that God's love is here now. Gradually, we learn to accept the love and claim it for ourselves."

Hogben believes that any ideas of separateness between people are tricks played on us by our limited consciousness. "Although our society is trying its best to deny it, we are whole people with spiritual as well as physical and mental natures. Spirituality plays a major role in some forms of healing within our society. However, many healing arts are not practiced with spiritual consciousness. This is unfortunate since healing that does not awaken the individual to the health-giving fire of God's Spirit is incomplete. Hopefully, the growing consciousness for living in the Spirit will develop our knowledge and acceptance of spirituality in the healing arts."

In Hogben I had found a medical scientist who blended the world of science and the spiritual world and found them compatible.

CHAPTER SEVEN ✿✿

W HILE MARIE COMEAU WAS PREPARING HER son Jeffrey's two favorite foods, mashed potatoes and cranberry sauce, for dinner in her Springfield, Massachusetts, kitchen in late 1983, he was in his room making up for the last two weeks of school, which he had missed. This would not be difficult for the eleven-year-old; Jeffrey was a regular on the honor roll. In fact, Marie was amazed that he could sit in front of the TV watching an entire evening's worth of sports on cable and still come home with straight As.

Although all Marie's children had been good students, Jeffrey seemed to have the most natural ability for learning. He could read something once, and it would be permanently fixed in his memory bank. One counselor called this ability a photographic memory. But in addition to being a bright child, he was also sensitive— perhaps too sensitive, Marie feared. She thought back to all the times Jeffrey had come home from school announcing that he no longer wanted to go back. He couldn't take the constant taunting—"a fat boy who can't do nothin'," they called him. They were referring to the fact that he was slightly overweight and was unable to participate in gym classes. Jeffrey had been born without arches in his feet. At an early age he had been put in leg braces to keep his knees from knocking together. The kids were unforgiving. While they kicked soccer balls, played touch football, and performed calisthenics, Jeffrey stood on the sidelines. Only for minutes at a time could he join in. One of the best memories Jeffrey had was one time when the soccer ball drifted over to where he was standing. In a split second, he mustered all his strength and kicked the ball soaring over all the kids' heads. Afterward, several in the class came up and told him that he was a "mean kicker." Jeffrey lived on that for weeks.

But those times were few and far between. They were not nearly frequent enough to sustain his sense of self-worth as he boarded the special "seated bus" that picked him up every day. He hated that special bus as much as he hated the ridicule; whenever possible Marie spared her son the agony and drove him to school. Regularly, she and Jeffrey had meetings with his teachers in an effort to ease the pain he was going through. The teachers loved Jeffrey and tried to explain that the kids would eventually outgrow their cruelty. They would remind Jeffrey how very special he was. But Jeffrey wasn't that interested in having his teachers think he was wonderful. He wanted the approval of his peers.

But now the problem of Jeffrey's flat arches was suddenly dwarfed by a bigger problem, a monumental problem. It all began a few months earlier when Jeffrey had complained that his legs and fingers were stiff. He began sleeping during the day and going to bed early. Marie, suspicious of the puffiness around Jeffrey's knuckles, felt that it was something more than the flu that had been going around. She took her son to a doctor. "Jeffrey never complains without a reason," she told Dr. Lawrence Zemel. He wasn't behaving normally. It just wasn't like Jeffrey to nap during the day and go to bed right after dinner.

Dr. Zemel examined Jeffrey. Then he sent him to the Wesson Memorial Hospital in Springfield for further testing. A week later, there was a diagnosis; it came so suddenly, so shockingly, that Marie was stunned. Jeffrey had bone cancer.

Marie refused to believe that this was her son's fate. It was simply unacceptable. She took him for a second opinion, this time to Springfield Hospital. The biopsy revealed the same thing: bone cancer. It was active. Jeffrey would have to undergo his first chemotherapy treatment the following week. Marie felt her entire world come crashing down.

Jeffrey did not seem to grasp the enormity of his condition. He didn't fully comprehend what bone cancer meant. And his mother didn't allow herself to tell him. As Marie prepared dinner in the kitchen that night, Jeffrey was in his room studying for an American history exam and anticipating homemade mashed potatoes and cranberry sauce. He looked up from reading about the Battle of Gettysburg and stared at the posters covering all four walls. Every sport from basketball to rugby was depicted on the huge colored prints. Ever since Jeffrey could remember, he had been obsessed with ending up on one of those posters himself one day. As soon as the pain in his legs went away and he got rid of his dumb orthopedic shoes and leg braces, he was sure he would be able to consistently kick soccer balls high over the other kids' heads. Then he would be permanently dubbed "the mean kicker."

Just the thought of that propelled Jeffrey to get up

from his desk and pick his football up off the floor. To do this, he had to manipulate his hands as if they belonged to a robot. In the last few weeks, he had no longer been able to hold anything. The back of his hand looked like a rubber ball. There were no knuckles to be seen. But that was only a temporary condition, Jeffrey consoled himself. The medicine that he would be taking—chemo-something-or-other—would take that away.

With the football tucked into his chest, he walked over to the mirror on his dresser. Taking off his glasses, he hunched his shoulders forward and quietly began to call out forward passes, Joe Namath style. As he did so, he heard his mother calling him to dinner.

Conversation at the table was forced, as it had been for the last two evenings, since Marie had first sat the family down and told them of Jeffrey's condition. Theresa, the eldest daughter, seemed to have taken the news the worst. A nursing student, she had seen children ravaged by the disease. Memories of bald children with rickety bodies playing feebly in the pediatric ward haunted her. Her baby brother had been through enough in his young life. This wasn't fair. She could not accept it.

Marie's own mother, who lived with them, was the strongest. As a devout Catholic, her faith did not allow her to believe for one moment that Jeffrey would not make it. Earlier that day, she had gone to church to light candles and pray for her grandson's recovery.

Although the family went to mass together on Sundays, Marie's faith had waned over the years. There were too many other things, more immediate, to think about. With no husband, she had to worry about keeping her four children fed, clothed, and educated. Education was at the top of her list. She prided herself that all her children were good students. None of them had ever gotten into trouble. None had ever taken drugs.

But now, as she passed around second helpings of chicken, thoughts of religion suddenly came back to her. Excusing herself from the dinner table, Marie went upstairs to her bedroom and searched through her handbag until she found what she had been looking for: It was a magazine she had picked up many months earlier at a healing service. It had been an unbelievable experience—a woman called Grace sang and performed healings. Marie thought back to the scores of people she had seen collapse when the woman touched their foreheads, and to the scores of people who actually claimed that they had been healed after being touched by her. At the time, it had all seemed so hard to believe that Marie hadn't even bothered to take the magazine out of her handbag and read it.

That had been her attitude months ago, before Jeffrey got sick. Now Marie flipped through the thin magazine in earnest. Maybe it *was* for real, she said to herself. And if it wasn't, they still would have nothing to lose by giving it a try. With only a shred of hope, Marie picked up the phone and dialed the twenty-four-hour prayer line. Minutes later, she was back downstairs. Scribbled on the back of the magazine were directions to Grace's next service.

At one o'clock the following afternoon, Jeffrey, Marie, and her mother left their home in Springfield. If everything went as scheduled, they would arrive at the junior high school in Danbury, Connecticut, four hours later. Marie wasn't taking any chances on being late. She allowed an hour and a half extra for getting lost, plus another hour for grabbing a bite of supper before the seven-thirty service.

Marie and her mother sat in the front seat; Marie drove. Jeffrey was sprawled out in the back. His head was propped up by two pillows. His legs were dangling halfway off the seat. The leg braces made it hard for him to get comfortable. Every so often, his grandmother would reach back to tuck the blanket around his legs to keep them from sliding off the seat as he slept.

At regular intervals, Jeffrey woke up from his nap. He wanted to know where they were and how much longer before they got there. But more important, he seemed to want to be reassured that this whole experience wasn't going to be too "weird."

"Do I have to tell the lady what's wrong with me in front of lots of people?" he asked.

Jeffrey was very shy in front of strangers. This concerned Marie; it was very likely that he wouldn't even go up for a healing. She had to be careful about what she told her son to expect. She certainly didn't want to offer him false hope by saying that if he went up for a healing, he would be sure to get better. But on the other hand, if Jeffrey didn't at least give it a try, nothing could happen.

"Does she call you by your name?" he wanted to know. "How does she know what's wrong with me? Do I tell her?"

Marie kept reassuring her son that she would be right there at his side to take him up if Grace should call on him. She also told him that if Grace laid hands on him and nothing happened, he was not to be upset.

"These things don't always work," Marie warned. "Sometimes it's fun to go and see these kinds of things happen to other people, just to experience it."

Marie was glad that they arrived at the junior high school early. The service wasn't for another half-hour, but the parking lot was already practically full. Because it was cold and the wind had started to blow, she dropped her mother and Jeffrey off near the main entrance, then went to find a parking space.

Jeffrey and his grandmother found three seats together in the center of the auditorium. As he took off his down jacket, he leaned toward his grandmother and said that it looked a lot like his own school auditorium. She took that as a sign that he felt somewhat at ease being there. He also seemed interested in seeing all those on crutches and in wheelchairs. "There's people here that are a lot worse than me, Grandma," Jeffrey whispered, glancing down at his swollen hands as if they were the extent of his problem.

Unable to force a comment along that line in return, she deftly combed her grandson's thick, sandy hair with her fingers. "It's about time for a haircut," she said. Her voice was strained and soft.

It was a quarter past seven. The service would begin in only fifteen minutes.

As Marie was entering the high school auditorium from the parking lot, Grace was backstage in a secluded corner behind the curtain, deep in prayer. For about an hour before every service, oblivious to the sound system tests and the ushers milling around, Grace quietly talked to God.

"Dear Lord, don't let anyone leave here tonight without knowing you. Make them whole in you. I love you, Lord. Lord, heal the blind, the deaf, the crippled. Heal those with cancer, the physically and mentally abused. Lord, heal the alcoholics, the drug dependent, the depressed."

107

Seated on a metal folding chair, Grace occasionally fell down to her knees, as if she were totally unaware that she was wearing a flowing chiffon gown. Lifting one arm toward the sky, sometimes both, she alternated talking to God in English and in Glossalalia, that strange, inexplicable phenomenon of speaking in tongues.

"Dear Lord, engulf me in your love. Let your love flow through me to heal and touch your people, so they might see the glory of God, and that any doubts and fears that they might have would be gone. Give me the compassion and the mercy of Jesus that I can feel for each one as Jesus would feel."

As she prayed, Larry James, the guitarist, crossed over to her and placed his hand over Grace's head. In only minutes, it would be time for him to go out on stage and introduce Grace to the audience.

"Use Grace for your glory," Larry said, as he lifted his hand in the air. "Speak through her, Jesus, the words you would like people to hear tonight. Give your words of knowledge, words of wisdom. Lord, we know that you've anointed Grace to do this, and we truly expect to see miracles and healings for your glory. Jesus, this is your service, may your will be done, not ours. But please don't let anyone leave here tonight without some blessing from God."

Then Larry picked up his guitar and walked out onto the stage. Grace had fallen back to her knees. She continued to be deep in prayer.

"Praise the Lord!" Larry called to the audience, as he adjusted the microphone on the left-hand side of the stage. Behind him, in the center of the stage, was a simple set design: a five-foot white cross with three baskets of fresh flowers at its base. "How many are

The photo of one-year-old Grace that won her a Gerber Baby prize

Grace at five years, attending a wedding

Grace's grandmother, Vacelia Tskanikas, who became a Greek Orthodox nun

Grace and Larry DiBiccari on their honeymoon

BELOW, *The DiBiccari children—Christopher, two and a half, Larry, four, and the twins Karen and Sharon, one and a half*

A recent family portrait

Grace with her mother, Antoinette Tskanikas

A crowd of about 4,000 attend a service at the County Center in White Plains, New York

Grace with her accompanists, Larry James and David Fields

Grace praying for members of the audience

A typical scene at a service

A man experiences a healing, lets go of his crutches, and testifies about it to the audience

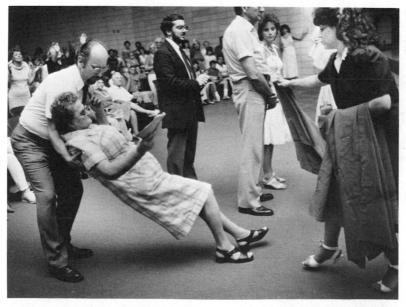

Grace's daughter Karen, who assists her mother at services, ready to cover a woman's legs once she is lying on the floor

At the Black, White and Free Gospel Concert and Parade, 1981.
FROM LEFT, *a local minister, then United States Congressman*
William Ratchford, Danbury Mayor James Dyer, and Grace

At a service

Tony DiBernardi, healed of lung cancer, shows his X-rays
to Grace

Jeffrey Comeau demonstrates a part of his cancer healing to
the audience. His mother, Marie, is at left.

Beatrice LaVasseur, who received a healing,
with her husband, Euclid

Nella Norbut, who was healed of liver cancer,
with her daughter, Andrea

Grace's father, George, steps forward to give his life to Jesus. This is the first time Grace had seen her father in many years.

Grace and her father at a service in 1984, one year after their reconciliation

here for the first time?" he wanted to know. About half the audience raised their hands. "Well, for those of you who haven't seen us before, we're called Grace 'N Vessels of Christ Ministries. We travel throughout the northeastern United States holding musical healing services. Everywhere we go, we see people being healed of such things as cancer, multiple sclerosis, deafness, drug addiction. And all these healings happen through the spirit of God. Grace is not the healer. Grace does not claim to be a healer. She claims that Jesus is the healer. It's as simple as that."

Larry was no stranger to audiences. He was articulate and congenial, with a way of speaking and appearance that were contagious and professional.

"Grace prays for people in the audience," Larry explained. "She is led to them by God. Tonight, you should not look to Grace for a healing—but to Jesus."

Larry went on to describe what would be happening in such a way that even a card-carrying atheist might be persuaded to hang around.

"You might be in the audience tonight not believing a word of what I just said. Well, I say, if you're a skeptic and don't believe there is a God—we're glad you're here. Because what you're going to see in the next three hours can change your life forever."

It was eight o'clock. Suddenly, it got warm—almost hot. The auditorium was packed. There were even people lined up along the sides and in the back. Marie helped Jeffrey pull off his wool sweater. Practically everyone was singing and clapping along with Larry as he led them in a song called "Lift Jesus Higher." The audience's mood seemed more like that of a country folk festival. Some people had their arms stretched in the air, waving in rhythm to the upbeat music. As they did, Marie caught a look in her mother's eye that silently announced that she could have done with a little less crowd enthusiasm.

Marie didn't mind either the wait or the enthusiasm. If it hadn't been for Jeffrey being so uncomfortable, she would have enjoyed the music. But his hands and legs were bothering him even more than usual. Marie told Jeffrey to sit down. He refused; he didn't want to draw attention to himself while everyone else was standing.

Then, just as Larry began strumming a new tune, Grace breezed out onto the stage, a picture of radiance and energy. She was singing "Hallelujah, Praise the Lord." Jeffrey, hearing the female voice, stood on his tiptoes, peeking between the heads in front of him, trying to get a look at this creature whom they had driven all afternoon to see.

"She's pretty," Jeffrey said, surprised. "Is that Grace?"

He had thought that Grace would look more like the elderly nuns sitting two rows in front of him. Instead, he saw an attractive woman in a bright red gown and long black hair ornamented with a flower. Although Marie's mother didn't comment on Grace's looks, she was thinking along the same lines as her grandson. In fact, Grace's uncommon good looks combined with her total ease in front of the audience aroused in Marie's mother a certain degree of suspicion. Even after she had heard several incredible testimonies of healings and had seen dozens of people topple over when Grace touched their foreheads, she still felt there was a gimmick somewhere. She was thinking that an afternoon in church, spent lighting candles and saying rosaries, would be more of a sure thing.

Marie's feelings were different. If only Grace would call on Jeffrey, something was bound to happen. Something *had* to happen. Perhaps it was just wishful thinking, but that was all she had left. For an hour, Grace walked up and down the aisles, plucking people apparently at random from their seats. Sometimes she went over to an area and called out the name of a disease. Invariably, someone would rise to claim it. Sometimes she went right up to a person and told what was wrong.

At one point, Grace came to the end of the row where the Comeaus were seated. With a thousand-mile stare, she scanned each person, stopping the longest on Jeffrey. At least, it appeared that way to Marie. But then Grace pointed to a man sitting next to Marie's mother and said, "Sir, you have colitis. You can't hold any food down. I want you to come forward for a healing."

The man was visibly shaken. He stumbled his way in front of their legs. Marie noticed that her mother looked equally shaken. Her hands were wrapped so tightly around thc arms of the chair that her knuckles were actually white. Jeffrey, on the other hand, was much more casual. After the humbling sensation of seeing the first dozen people or so topple over, he began to detach himself emotionally, assuming the role of detective to try to figure out how all this was happening.

While Marie silently prayed for Grace to call on her son, Jeffrey regularly interrupted her with various theories. At first he had no doubt that the anointing oil into which Grace dipped her fingers was laced with ether or chloroform. Obviously, a chemical was causing people to pass out. But after further observation, he had to drop that theory; there was no pungent odor, and there were too many times when she didn't use the oil, yet people still passed out. Or a subject would topple when Grace pointed a finger at them from eight or ten feet away. His next theory was similar to the children's game Chicken, in which one kid would close his eyes and another would come up close and try to frighten him into falling backward. Jeffrey whispered to his mother that when they got home he would show her how it was done.

At nearly ten o'clock, Grace announced that anyone who hadn't already been prayed for and who wanted a healing should line up along the sides of the auditorium. One-fourth of the audience got up. Just as Marie had expected, Jeffrey declined to go up. However, Grace had said that if anyone wanted a prayer for someone who couldn't be there, they should go up themselves and bring a handkerchief. Fortunately, Marie had one in her handbag; she went over to the side of the auditorium.

Marie hadn't been standing in the line for more than ten minutes when Grace suddenly broke away from the healing procession. "There's a young boy here tonight," Grace said, "with bone cancer."

Marie felt faint. She could barely take in Grace's next words. She was saying something about a young man who was still seated. It had to be Jeffrey. And Marie had to get out of the line and tell him that he must go up for a healing. She started back to her seat, but she couldn't find her row. Finally she spotted her mother. She was sitting alone. Jeffrey wasn't there. He must have been frightened of being called out and left the hall. Marie motioned to her mother that she was going to look for him in the back when she suddenly heard Grace say, "We're going to pray for your cancer to go away."

Jeffrey was up there with Grace. "How'd you get him

to go?" Marie asked, a little too loudly, as she sat down next to her mother.

"I didn't," she whispered. "He just went right up when she called him."

Marie clutched her mother's hand. It was moist, just like her own. Together their hearts were racing. Marie thought she could actually hear their pulses pounding through their locked fingers.

"We're going to pray for the cancer to go away, for you to be all well again," Grace whispered into Jeffrey's ear. Her one arm was wrapped tightly around his shoulders. Her hand was resting on his forehead.

For Jeffrey, the five hundred people watching were no longer strangers. They hadn't been, from the moment Grace's words had registered: "There's a young boy here tonight with bone cancer. You're still seated." Going forward for a healing was an act as natural as going to the dinner table when his mother called him. The people all around him were people just like himself, people with needs. They were not laughing at his orthopedic shoes. They were not staring at the way he walked. No one was going to shout out, "The fat boy who can't do nothin'!" No one was going to gawk at his puffed-up hands that looked like softballs sewn onto his wrists.

"Dear God," Grace began, "take this cancer from this little boy's body. Make him whole again in you."

Jeffrey had long since dismissed his thoughts about trying to get a sample of that anointing oil. Now, with Grace's hand on his forehead, he couldn't concentrate on anything except the strange, comfortable feeling that was coming over him. He began to feel warm; it was an inner warmth, as if he had just come in from the cold and had downed a mug of hot chocolate. The feeling ran from his head to his toes. Something was happening. His fingers and toes tingled, as if they had fallen asleep and were just waking up.

Grace was massaging his fingers, which only minutes ago couldn't even be touched lightly. Now there was no pain, just a tingling sensation.

"Move your fingers," Grace said.

Slowly and cautiously, Jeffrey opened and closed his hands. The puffiness was disappearing. It was as if someone had suddenly loosened the neck of a balloon and it was deflating. Within minutes, his fingers were as limber as they had been two years ago, when he had played the saxophone.

Jeffrey continued to open and close his hands, feeling as if he were discovering the miracle of fingers for the first time. Grace was at this side, her arm wrapped around his shoulders.

"Jesus just healed this young man!" she called out to the audience, her eyes glistening. "How do you feel?" she said, turning to Jeffrey.

Suddenly and unexpectedly, Jeffrey lifted his voice and shouted, "I've got no pain! Mommy, I've got no *pain*!" He jumped up and down, testing both his fingers and his legs.

The audience was used to seeing miracles. So far that night, two people had left their wheelchairs. Several had claimed to be healed of deafness and glaucoma. Arthritics, alcoholics, and drug addicts also claimed to have been delivered. But the audience had seen nothing as dramatic as what had just happened to Jeffrey Comeau. Excitement permeated the auditorium. Jeffrey continued to jump up and down, repeating "I've got no pain." Everyone was standing in celebration. The audience joined in as Grace belted out "I've Got the Faith."

Marie and her mother were afraid to acknowledge the incredible scene that had just taken place. They feared that at any moment they might awaken to the cold reality that this hadn't really happened. They sat there stiff and dreamlike. It was hours before they could take in what had happened.

The following Monday morning, nobody in the Comeau home needed an alarm clock. Marie got up at six to make a special pancake breakfast for the second day in a row. As the bacon sizzled, she jotted down quick notes on what she would say to Jeffrey's doctor when it came time to phone him. Jeffrey had been up since five-thirty, lying in bed tossing a football up in the air and catching it with one hand. His grandmother had gone to seven o'clock mass. She wanted to thank God for the miracle and say a few more prayers as a backup.

After breakfast, Jeffrey cleared the table. He did so with one hand, dribbling a basketball with the other. Marie loaded the last of the plates into the dishwasher. Then she looked at the kitchen clock. It was nine o'clock—time to call Jeffrey's doctor. She wanted privacy. It would be difficult enough, she thought, to explain to him what had happened to her son without her well-intentioned mother giving hand signals two inches from the phone, trying to coach her on what to say, which she was likely to do. And then there was Jeffrey. Every time the phone had rung in the last twenty-four hours, Jeffrey had grabbed it to tell whoever called how his knuckles had grown right in front of his eyes. Although that is exactly what had happened, Marie wanted to keep it low-key for the doctor.

As it turned out, Marie had to go through a clumsy explanation for the nurse before she was put through to Dr. Zemel. When he finally did get on the line, Marie was careful to leave out the word *miracle.* As soberly as possible, she gave the doctor the facts. But the facts were incredible: A woman touched Jeffrey's forehead; minutes later his hands deflated to their normal size; his legs straightened; the pain left.

Because this must have sounded absolutely incredible, Marie was not offended when Dr. Zemel made no comment and asked no further questions. He merely wanted to know if she could bring Jeffrey into his office at eleven o'clock. Marie hung up, feeling slightly foolish. However, that feeling would pass the moment the doctor saw Jeffrey, she was sure of that.

At the doctor's office, Marie approached the slot in the sliding-glass window. "Jeffrey Comeau here for an eleven o'clock appointment with Dr. Zemel," she said.

"Just have a seat," responded the nurse. "The doctor will be with you shortly."

As Marie turned toward the magazine rack, she wondered if this was the same nurse she had spoken to earlier in the day. She had a distinct feeling that it was. She felt that the nurse was peering out from behind the glass with a half-smirk. Marie checked herself: she wasn't going to get paranoid over the look a nurse gave her. This paranoia was probably all in her own imagination, anyway. Marie was sensitive to how others felt about miracles; she herself had felt that same way— before Saturday night, that is. Perhaps it was her own skepticism surfacing, and she was now projecting it onto the nurse. As much as Marie wanted to believe that a full-blown miracle had happened, doubts still cropped up.

There was no denying that something remarkable had happened to her son. It was physical; you couldn't ignore it. But there were thoughts that troubled her. Was this healing of the outer symptoms indicative of what had gone on inside? Had the bone cancer gone away along with the puffiness and the pain? She didn't know. Only a doctor could determine this.

Jeffrey was too excited even to read the latest *Sports Illustrated*. He dug a tennis ball out of his jacket pocket and squeezed it in the palm of his hand. A middle-aged man sitting across from them asked Marie if her son had just gotten a cast off his arm and was strengthening his muscles. Marie looked up from her magazine, smiled, and said no. He had had a bone problem, she said. Jeffrey wouldn't let the story die there. He proceeded to tell that man and three other patients about the miracle. As he got into the vivid details about how his knuckles had grown, part of Marie felt like burying her face in the magazine she was reading. But the other part of her was proud of the way her son was suddenly so willing to talk to perfect strangers.

Before Jeffrey had the chance to repeat his story for two new people who had just come in, the nurse called them into the examining room. Dr. Zemel came in behind them. Without acknowledging that he and Marie had spoken earlier, he picked up Jeffrey's hands and inspected them, both front and back. Silently, he pressed each finger, twisting and turning it.

"Does that hurt?" he asked Jeffrey over the tops of his half-lenses.

"No, sir, it doesn't."

Marie had asked Jeffrey on the drive over not to mention anything about what had happened unless the doctor asked.

Dr. Zemel continued pressing the joints, manipulating Jeffrey's legs, fingers, wrists, and ankles. There was no mention of how the swelling had suddenly disappeared. The only discussion between Jeffrey and the doctor was about who would win the NFL playoffs and about how Joe Namath would probably go down as the best quarterback in history.

"Okay, sport," Dr. Zemel said to Jeffrey, patting him on the back. "I want you to go down the hall with the nurse for some blood work."

But before Jeffrey slid off the examining table, he said, "Mom, ask Dr. Zemel about you-know-what."

Marie had promised Jeffrey that if the doctor gave the go-ahead, she would buy him what he had been dying for: a pair of Pro-X 100 sneakers.

Dr. Zemel inspected Jeffrey's feet and legs once again. He asked him to stand, walk, get on his tiptoes, hop on one leg, and rock backward and forward before he finally said, "There's enough of an improvement. I think we can give those Pro-X's a shot. But don't throw away the leg braces," he added. "We'll try you without them and see what happens."

Those words were magical to Jeffrey. It was the first time in his life that he would be out of orthopedic shoes and braces. "Now I can be a big shot just like the other guys at school," Jeffrey said as he left the examining room.

Dr. Zemel picked up Jeffrey's medical chart, turned to Marie, and asked her to follow him down to his office.

"I don't understand this," he said, sinking into a large black chair behind a cluttered desk. "It's certainly nothing I've done."

"Does this mean the bone cancer is gone?" Marie said, almost reluctant to ask.

"We won't know that," he said, rolling a pen between his thumb and forefinger, "until we run some more tests."

Carefully, he reviewed Jeffrey's chart. "Just four days ago," he said, "your son was diagnosed as having active bone cancer. I must warn you, Mrs. Comeau, that it is very unlikely that it has gone into a remission."

"But you just examined him. You saw what happened to his hands!" Marie said, choking back tears. "Couldn't something miraculous have happened on the inside as well?" She hadn't intended to use that word, but now she no longer cared.

"Something out of the ordinary has occurred," he said. "But I'm a medical man. I'm not trained to think that way. I don't believe in miracles."

Arrangements were made for Jeffrey to go into the hospital the following morning for more tests. If the tests came back negative, Jeffrey would be home free and clear. But Dr. Zemel doubted very much that they would, he told Marie. It was highly probable that Jeffrey would begin his first chemotherapy treatment on schedule.

When Marie left the doctor's office, her emotions ran from optimism to deep despair. For Jeffrey's sake, she tried to share his excitement as they went to a string of different shoestores in search of the Pro-X 100's. The fourth store had Jeffrey's size. He wore them home. His feet barely touched the cement.

The biospy would not be in for three days. Until that time, Marie put her life on hold.

Marie looked at her watch. It was four-thirty in the afternoon. In a half-hour, Dr. Zemel would phone with the results of Jeffrey's tests for bone cancer. Too anxious to wait any longer, Marie dialed the doctor's office.

The nurse put her on hold. A few minutes later, the nurse got back on. The results had just come in. She was unable to give her the information, but she promised that the moment the doctor finished with his last patient, he would phone. She thought it would be around five o'clock.

The past three days had been the longest in Marie's life. If the tests were negative, it meant—at least to her—that a miracle had really happened. If the tests were positive, Jeffrey would begin chemotherapy treatments the following day. Marie had to keep reminding herself that she must be prepared either way, just as, earlier in the day, she had tried to prepare Jeffrey.

"Jeffrey," Marie said as he headed out the back door, a football tucked underneath his arm, "the doctor is going to call today. We'll know if you have to start taking the chemotherapy or not."

"Mommy, look at me!" He tossed the football up into the air with one hand and caught it with the other. "You call that sick?"

Marie watched Jeffrey from the kitchen window. He was kicking the football so high in the air that she could barely see where it went. Tears filled her eyes just thinking about what a positive report would do psychologically for her son. With his leg braces off, sporting his new Pro-X 100's, he was part of the gang. As Marie diced carrots and celery for a salad, she prayed to God for one last miracle: a negative bone scan.

At last the phone rang.

"Mrs. Comeau," Dr. Zemel said. "I don't understand this, but all of Jeffrey's tests came back negative."

For a fraction of a second, Marie wasn't sure if negative meant that the cancer was gone, or that it was negative news.

"Negative—?" Marie said tentatively.

"There's not a trace of cancer to be found in your son."

"It's a miracle!" Marie blurted out. She no longer cared if the doctor believed in miracles or not.

On the other end of the line, the doctor listened silently as Marie, once again, related the story of the evening Jeffrey was healed.

After a polite length of time listening, he said that he would be keeping a close eye on Jeffrey. Then he put his nurse on the phone to schedule a check-up appointment for the following month. He made no comment about what Marie considered to be a miracle healing.

After Marie hung up, she went into Jeffrey's room. She tried to tell him the good news, but all that came out were tears. Jeffrey, however, had never doubted that he was healed. His only comment was, "Mom, I told you, Jesus healed me. You always sweat the small stuff."

A year later, I met with Jeffrey and his family. They had driven from Springfield down to Danbury to attend one of Grace's services. Earlier in the week, we had arranged to meet in the high school corridor a half hour before the service. For some reason, I was looking for a skinny twelve-year-old kid. Instead, a tall, husky young man who towered over my five-foot-three-inches introduced himself as Jeffrey Comeau. Standing next to him was his mother, an attractive, petite woman, and his grandmother and his two sisters.

We stood around chatting for at least fifteen minutes before there was any mention of the word *cancer*. Jeffrey and my husband were talking about the New York

Mets. I was talking with the others about everything but Jeffrey's miraculous healing.

Five minutes before the service was to begin, I interrupted the baseball talk. "Jeffrey, you look fantastic," I said. "How do you feel?"

Jeffrey turned to his mother. "Mom, you tell Mrs. Fuller the news."

For a second, I felt as if my heart were going to stop. But the moment I saw Marie's eyes light up, I was certain that everything was okay.

"It's been one year today with absolutely no sign of cancer, anywhere. And just yesterday—"

Jeffrey didn't let his mother finish. "Just yesterday I got this doctor's report," he said. He took a crumpled piece of paper from his jeans and handed it to me. "It says right here: 'All cancer biopsy negative.' But the best part," he said, pointing to the bottom of the medical report, "is where it says I can now participate in all sports at school! See that? I'm perfect." He kicked out his leg like a soccer player.

When he did that, I looked down and noticed that he was wearing a pair of Pro-X 100's.

CHAPTER EIGHT ❧❧

TWO YEARS EARLIER, IN DECEMBER 1982, FATHER Rousso was administering Holy Communion in the living room of Beatrice and Euclid LeVasseur. Afterward, over a leisurely cup of coffee, he would do what he had done the first Friday of every month for the past year: chat with the couple and fill them in on what was going on around the parish. Both Beatrice and her husband missed being able to attend Sunday and holiday masses and all the social functions at the church.

Ever since Beatrice's last unsuccessful operation to connect her prolapsed intestine to her spine, she had been unable to leave the house. The doctor had told her quite simply that he could do nothing more to correct the situation. If he operated again, he would have to perform a colostomy. Beatrice was reluctant to rush into more surgery. In the last three years, she had had eight operations. There had been no improvement.

This particular Friday morning, however, Euclid LeVasseur had made up his mind to ask Father Rousso about a woman called Grace. His son had been constantly encouraging his parents to go see the healer ever since the cancerous tumors of a relative had disappeared at a service. Euclid wasn't inclined to believe in such things, but the way Beatrice had been feeling lately, he wondered if his son might have a point—they had nothing to lose.

"It's funny you ask," Father Rousso said. "Just the other day, someone else from the church asked about Grace."

The priest went on to say that he had done preliminary checking and felt that Grace was doing nothing that could be construed as sacrilegious. "If you do go," the priest warned, "remember that when Jesus was on earth, He didn't heal everyone. But I know your faith is too great to be hurt if you don't get healed."

On the way out the door, the priest popped his head back into the room and quickly added, "Make sure you go!"

That was all the LeVasseurs needed to hear. They phoned their son and made arrangements to be taken to the next service. Because of her excruciating pain and hemorrhaging that developed on the day of the service, Beatrice had to lie on a mattress in the back of her son's jeep for the hour's ride.

Two years later, I talked with Beatrice LeVasseur. She was a plump, pleasant lady with an engaging smile. Over tea, she told me what had happened at the service that night.

"There's a woman right here in this row," Grace had said, approaching and making eye contact with Beatrice, "with unbearable stomach pain. Come forward. Jesus wants to heal you."

Beatrice knew she was the one. But for some reason, she couldn't even make a gesture to get up. "I sat there too stunned to even raise my hand," Beatrice told me. "But I knew that she knew that it was I. She didn't take her eyes off me."

"I want the lady over there in the blue print dress to come up here," Grace said. Her voice was soft but firm.

Beatrice moved slowly and cautiously into the aisle.

"The instant Grace made a cross on my forehead with her fingers," Beatrice said, "I felt a power, an energy entering my head. I felt faint. But it wasn't a sick sort of fainting. There was a warmth that flooded me as I fell backward on the floor. When I came to, I tried to move to get up. I couldn't. One of the ushers was right there. He went to help me. But Grace saw him and said, 'Don't touch her, Jesus isn't through with her yet.'

"And then she came and prayed over me again. Again, I went out. When I came to, I still felt as if I were floating. I don't remember anything while I was out. I don't even know how long I was lying there. My husband thought it was at least five minutes. I just felt that warmth going through me. Finally, Grace leaned over and asked how I felt. She said that Jesus was all through with me and I could get up. I got up with no trouble. It was as if I were a three-year-old child. Before, I would have had to move first to my hands and knees.

"Then we started walking, then running. I was running up and down the aisles with Grace. The music was going. It was as if I had wings. My family was all sitting there crying. At the end of the service, I went into the bathroom and took off the protection I wore for my incontinence, and never put it back on again. Dr. Kurien was completely puzzled."

Then Beatrice added, "Perhaps you could talk to him to find out what he thinks."

I quickly arranged to do so. A firm medical opinion was obligatory.

"Obviously, something physical has happened to Beatrice LeVasseur," Dr. Abraham Kurien told me during an interview in his office. "But I warn you about making the distinction between physical and mental. Those are words that we have created. The Western view of reality is that it is dualistic. There is man. There is God. There is earth. There is heaven. To my point of view, this is all wrong. Reality is one. It is continuous. To me, there is no distinction between mental and physical. Those are words. And I think that that is where a lot of our confusion comes from. Is that a physical healing or is that a mental healing? To me, it is a healing. Period.

"I have no trouble accepting that a healing has taken place outside the frame of reference of scientific medicine. I think that medicine is not truly scientific if it denies the validity of what happens, because we basically have to accept facts. If someone has been healed, such as Mrs. LeVasseur, we must first accept that fact—even within the context of medicine itself. We often have a situation where a patient all of a sudden gets better. I think that if we're good scientists, we should take the fact for what it is and then try to explain it. And if you cannot explain it within the categories we have now, you then have to suspend judgment about it. And you say, okay, maybe science cannot explain it today.

"But maybe we'll find the explanation fifteen, twenty years from now. Because that is the basic nature of science. It does not pass judgment and deny facts. Science cannot simply say that something like this does not exist. That's not good science. That is being dogmatic, to say this did not happen when it has. Or that this could not have happened. Or else you say that the patient did not have a problem. And you may be tempted to say what looks like a miracle is 'diagnostic error.' Even in a good medical environment one recognizes that there are diagnoses made which are perfectly accurate, but then the pathology is not there awhile later. We cannot go back and say that the diagnosis was wrong. We can simply say that something has happened here that we do not understand. Those who are religious, such as this woman Grace, may say that a miracle has happened. But I feel that we should simply accept the fact that someone gets better. To me, my goal is that the patient should be well. I don't want them to have the feeling of well-being through things that are unscientific, i.e., 'quack medicine,' because it might do them harm. But I certainly wouldn't mind if a person went to a religious healing service and got better. I believe the view of science is not to become another religion. Science has to be all-comprehensive. It cannot isolate itself to a corner and say that everything not within this framework is inaccurate. Ultimately, I don't think that there is a conflict between science and religion. There may be conflicts between scientific theories and individual religions. I think that is what a lot of people are talking about—that this particular theory of science does not fit in with this particular understanding of reality in a given religion."

I was impressed with Dr. Kurien. He was cautious, direct, and sincere. He accepted what appeared to be an impossible healing on the basis that it had clearly happened, and happened without any scientific or medical explanation.

Dr. Kurien's appraisal brought to mind another case that I had checked into in considerable detail. A woman named Liz Thomas had been suffering from lupus, a collagen disease that affects the connective tissues. Nearly ten years after she had first been diagnosed with it at two major Boston hospitals, her husband was driving to the post office when he heard Grace being interviewed over the car radio. She was talking about all the medically documented healings that had occurred through her ministry.

More out of desperation for his wife's failing health than out of actual faith in miracle healings, Mr. Thomas swung off the road leading to the post office and headed toward the local radio station in the hope that it was a live show and not a tape.

As he walked into the radio station's waiting room, Grace and Larry James were walking out.

"Excuse me, ma'am," Mr. Thomas said, trying to remain calm. "I've never asked any favors from strangers before. But I need your help."

He went on to explain to Grace that his wife had just gotten out of the hospital the day before. The doctors couldn't do anything more for her. It was killing him and his children to see their once-active mother turning into a vegetable.

Although Grace had a newspaper interview scheduled, she turned to Larry and asked if he would phone the paper to see if she could do a phone interview so she could stay at the radio station. Mr. Thomas went home and returned with his wife.

"I didn't tell my wife where I was taking her," Mr. Thomas told me when I talked with him three years later. "I just got out her heavy winter coat, wool hat, and scarf, took them into the bedroom, and helped her put them on over her nightgown. I told her I'd explain in the car. But once I got her into the car, I was afraid that if I told her about Grace, she might refuse to see her. Instead, I just said that I was taking her to get help and to please trust me. Frankly, she was too sick and weak even to ask any questions."

Liz Thomas, a strikingly attractive middle-aged woman, recalled, "As Grace prayed over me at the radio station, I felt as if something had entered my body. It went right through me, and I collapsed onto the floor in front of the receptionist and two disc jockeys. At that time, I didn't even know anything about Grace or healers. And I certainly didn't know about 'falling out in the Spirit.' Now, whenever I hear people say that it's the power of suggestion that makes people fall backward, I have to correct them. Because I had absolutely no suggestion. As far as I knew, my husband could have been taking me to the radio station because we were instant Lotto winners." Liz laughed.

"In one way, we did win the lottery," she quickly added. "From the day Jesus healed me through Grace, I began to get progressively stronger. In one week I went from being bedridden to cleaning my own house and cooking the meals."

I asked Liz Thomas what her doctor's thoughts were.

"When I went back to the doctor," Liz said, "he reexamined me and then simply said that I never had had lupus disease, even though I had been diagnosed as having it at two separate hospitals. His medical mind apparently did not allow for miracles. It was more acceptable to say that I was misdiagnosed."

Listening to Liz Thomas, it was obvious that her doctor was not from the same school of thought as Beatrice LeVasseur's, Dr. Kurien. Dr. Kurien had no trouble accepting that there are those who get healed outside conventional medicine. He did not try to force what had happened into the mold of a wrong diagnosis or a spontaneous remission.

Months into this research, I decided I needed help. Medical help. I needed to find a physician who would come to a service and try to make sense out of what was happening. After considerable thought, I decided to ask Robert Madison, who was associate chief of staff at the Stamford Hospital in Connecticut and was in private practice as well. Two years earlier, he had been helpful in reviewing medical facts for a book I had written. Of course, that book had nothing to do with unconventional phenomena. I wasn't really sure what his attitude would be now.

I phoned his home one night and explained as rationally as I could all about Grace. When I told him that she just touches people and nearly half fall over, he called his wife, Marian, and told her to get on an extension. Marian teaches English literature at Fairfield University and has a sharp, inquiring mind. Together they listened as I described several of the more dramatic healings I had witnessed. Finally, Bob spoke.

"Well, Liz," he said wryly, "if they're out there, you'll find them."

"Don't pay any attention to him," Marian said. "This sounds fascinating! When can we go?"

"I thought you'd never ask." I told them that Grace was having a service in New Rochelle the following weekend, just a half-hour away from where they lived.

"Great," Marian said. "Come here and have something to eat, and we'll drive down together."

It seemed somewhat strange to be sitting in the front

row at Grace's service with a medical doctor. It must have seemed even stranger to Bob and Marian. As much as I had tried to explain over dinner what to expect, they were still unprepared. Several times, when someone began to topple in front of Bob, he lurched forward out of his seat with arms extended to help the usher gently lower the person to the floor. Occasionally he would stare down at whoever was lying at his feet, as if at any moment he were going to give a karate chop to the breastbone and begin CPR.

It was hard to tell what he thought. Before the healings started, both he and Marian had appeared to be enjoying themselves. They sang and clapped and even chuckled at the account that a man calling himself Bruno the Butcher gave about how he had been healed.

"There's a rough, tough man here tonight," Grace had said when she called on Bruno at his first service. "He only came because his wife wanted him to."

"I stayed way in the back because I don't believe in that stuff," Bruno now said into the microphone Grace was holding. He was a stocky man with a thick New York accent. "I thought that this was a money-making business. I said that she's a good businesswoman. She knows how to get people to dump money in the hat. But then as I'm sitting there, she comes up and picks me out as having arthritis in the shoulder. And she pointed out that it was in my back and all the way down the right side. How did she know that I had arthritis in the right shoulder?" he asked, throwing out his hands.

"She said that I should come forward for a healing. I get up and I'm still sort of laughing. Thinking, what could she do to me? She begins praying. I begin to laugh, thinking this is sort of silly. And the next thing I know

I'm down on my knees. I say, Bruno, what happened? Are you slipping? I get back up again and say, never. Then she knocks me down again. Before I know it—nobody touched me—I'm flat on my back. So flat you wouldn't believe it. I can't move. I ask, who's holding me down? Everybody starts laughing. But this is not a laughing matter. I cannot get up. All of a sudden I am, like, relieved. There is air. I rise up, and I can move all my joints."

Bruno wrapped up his testimony by saying that before encountering Grace, he could not lift his right arm. He could not even bring his butcher knife down onto a piece of meat. But after Grace's touch, he could move his arm in any way without pain.

As Bruno walked back to his seat, I asked Bob what he thought. He ran his fingers through his thick head of wavy silver hair and said, "Beats me."

"You believe it?" I asked.

"*Something* happened to him."

"You should go up for a healing," I said. "Get your ribs fixed." When John and I had arrived at their house, Marian had said that Bob had slipped two days earlier. He thought he had broken his ribs. They were bruised and painful.

"What if one of my patients sees me here?" he asked with a grin.

Grace was now walking over from the center of the auditorium to the right side, where we were seated. She stood directly in front of Bob. The tips of their shoes practically met. "If you're taking pills, don't go off them. First go back to your doctor. You go *back* to your doctor," she said forcefully. "Let him tell you that you don't need them. Amen."

It was a strange coincidence that Grace said all that

just two inches from Bob. I hadn't told her that we were bringing a doctor. I made it a point not to tell her anything about the friends I brought to see her. That way, if she happened to give one of them a personal message (as she often did), I would be able to check how accurate she was.

The last friend she had given a message to was Lester Osterman, the Broadway producer of such recent hits as *The Shadow Box* and *Da*. During the entire service, he had sat there trying to figure out whether it was merely hypnosis. He couldn't decide. At the end of the evening, Grace glided by Lester, stopping only long enough to whisper in his ear, "It's not hypnosis." Lester was taken by surprise. He hadn't even told his wife that that was what he had been thinking.

Now, after Grace said "Amen," I thought she was going to break out into a song. But she didn't. She was determined to make her point. "God and man work together," she said. "If you need a doctor, go to one. It's like some people who have no teeth. Or they have a whole lot missing, and they say, 'Well, God will fix 'em.' And they keep their toothless mouths open and say, 'God will grow teeth.' Well, I'm here to tell those people that there are dentists out there. So go get a set. Amen.

"I do believe," she added, "that if you need a tooth or if you have a bad cavity, and there aren't any dentists around, that God will help. But there are some people who go totally off the wall and get all ridiculous," Grace said, flashing a mouth full of white teeth.

"So remember," Grace added, "God and man work together. Before you go off your medication, check with your doctor. Got that? Praise God!" Then Grace moved down the aisle singing "Healing Hands."

133

"Liz," Bob asked the moment Grace began to sing, "did you tell her that I'm a doctor?"

"No," I said.

"Come on," he said, adjusting his steel-frame glasses, "you must have told her."

I had to admit that it did appear that way. Not only had she stood in front of him the entire time she spoke about doctors, but several times she had looked him squarely in the face.

"Whatever God has for you tonight," Grace said to the audience when she finished her song, "be open to a healing. I can't do anything for you. And I don't claim to. I pray. God called me to do that. His power, as many of you have witnessed, comes down upon us and runs through us."

Suddenly a woman stood up in the center of the auditorium. Flailing her arms, she screamed hysterically that Jesus was coming. This was the first time I had ever seen anyone lose control. I thought to myself, why did this have to happen with Bob and Marian here? Grace did not tolerate hysterics.

"That's enough of that!" Grace said firmly.

The woman immediately quieted. And Grace continued as if nothing had happened.

I remembered Grace telling me, when I had asked her if this kind of incident was a common event, that it only happened once in a great while. "If you don't put any energy into their outbreaks," Grace explained, "they'll quiet right down." But then Grace went on to tell me about a thirteen-year-old girl's outburst that nearly caused complete chaos.

"We were doing a service in a small New England town," Grace said. "I was coming down the healing line when all of a sudden I approached a young girl who began to make growling-like utterances. Her face was twisted. Her lips were wet. Foamy. I went to place my hand to her forehead and say, 'Be healed in the name of Jesus.' When I did, she came at me like some kind of wild, injured animal, making guttural noises. She was trying to claw my face.

"The ushers, noticing what was happening, grabbed her. Four of these big, huge men tried to hold her down, but they couldn't. She began to spin like a child's top. Her strength was inhuman."

Grace said that to make matters worse, the audience had become hysterical over what they were seeing. Her first responsibility was to keep control of the thousand people, or else all havoc could break out.

"I told the audience loud and clear," Grace said, "to sit down and be quiet. And to pray quietly for this girl. In that instant, the room silenced, which seemed to make things even more dramatic.

"The only thing you could hear was the girl's animal sounds. It was very eerie. I thought I had seen it all, up until that night. I quickly said, 'God, what's happening? What should I do?'

"Suddenly I felt as if God had put me inside a protective bubble. I just knew that that was my sign from Him that I shouldn't back off. God was showing me that this young girl was literally possessed. I couldn't back off and let the devil have his way. I had to confront Satan. And I had to do it right then and there.

" 'Jesus loves you! And I love you!' I kept saying. Each time I said that, she would scream, 'I hate you. Go away. I hate you!' But I knew that it would only be a matter of time before God overpowered the devil. The louder she screamed that she hated God and me, the louder I refuted. But finally we won. She threw

135

herself into my arms and cried, confessing that something beyond her control had hold of her. Earlier in the day, she had tried to kill herself. Her wrist was all bandaged."

Before the girl returned to her seat, she sang "Amazing Grace." She had a beautiful lyrical voice, and today she is singing in her church choir.

No such violence was taking place tonight—although for a moment I thought the hysterical woman was going to continue. She didn't.

Calm and assured, Grace said, "In a few minutes I'm going to ask those of you who haven't received healings and want one to come up to do so. But before that, I just want to remind you that it's not necessary to fall back to be healed. Some people are healed in their seats. Some are healed on the way home. Some are healed in the shower."

I was getting ready to ask Bob if he was going to go up to see if she could do anything for his ribs, when I noticed him poking at his ribcage. I thought that the two and a half hours we had been sitting had aggravated his condition.

"Why don't you go up?" I asked. "Maybe she can help?"

"I don't have to," he said with a peculiar expression.

"What do you mean?"

"They're not sore anymore," he said.

"What's not sore?" I asked.

"My ribs."

"You're joking."

"I don't believe in any of this stuff." He shook his head. "But the pain is gone."

"You're really serious?" I asked.

"I can't believe it," he said, still shaking his head.

Once we got settled back into the car and were on

our way home, I asked the Madisons what they thought.

"Well, it takes time for it to sink in," Marian said. "It's the first time I've ever experienced anything like that."

Before Bob even spoke, I knew that Marian was going to have a more open outlook than he. Perhaps her background as a professor allowed for a more liberal attitude.

"Okay, number one," Bob said as he rolled the window down. "First of all, she has an extraordinary personality. She has a forceful approach to people, using repetition and religion."

"She believes in what she's doing," Marian said.

"Yes," Bob said. "She's no phony. But on the other hand, who are the people who are going to this thing? People who go to these things are believers."

"Not all of them," I said, reminding him of Bruno the Butcher and several others we heard give testimonies.

"Eighty percent are," he cut in. "If I saw an advertisement in the paper to go see Grace the healer, there would be no way I'd ever go."

"How are your ribs feeling?" I asked.

"Good," he said as he poked at them quickly. Then he went on. "You're dealing with a specific audience. Except for a few nonbelievers who were there, they're all believers. They come there because they're religious. They believe in Jesus. They believe in miracles. They believe in God."

"You believe in God?" I asked, already knowing the answer.

"No."

"The more biochemists study, the more they get to the theory that there is a being—a creative force," Marian said.

"I don't believe in the supernatural," Bob continued.

"I believe in the power of the brain and the will to live."

"Do you believe in Sir John Eccles's theory about the mind being separate from the brain? He's a Nobel Prize winner," John wanted to know.

"Yeah, the brain is a physical, chemical machine, and the mind is what you do with it," Bob replied.

"The mind is the software and the brain is the hardware?" John asked.

"Well, that's a good analogy," Bob agreed.

"Back to Grace" I said.

"I think she's terrific. She's a good person. I wouldn't knock her for a minute," Bob said. "She's charismatic. A top-notch show performer."

"You think that it's just a show?" I asked.

"I didn't say that. I'm not saying she's just a show. She means what she's doing."

"I feel the same way as Bob about that," Marian said. "But I don't know how people were getting healed. As I said before, I have to let this all sink in."

"Bob," I asked, "do you believe that legitimate healings were actually taking place?"

"Absolutely," he said. "That's what's so terrific about her."

"How do you think that happens?"

"It's all the power of the mind," he said, in a matter-of-fact way. "People who go up want to be healed. They believe that Jesus is going to heal them."

"What about the skeptics?" I asked.

"I don't think there were any there."

"What about you?"

"What about me?" he asked, breaking out into a grin.

"You're a skeptic. And you said your ribs no longer hurt."

"That's right," he said, but changed the track of the conversation. "She's magnificent. If she can get somebody off drugs, off alcohol, that's great. If she can get all the thousands of people who are depressed and can say to them, 'Jesus is going to enter your body, and depression is going to leave,' and they believe in it, then she's worth a fortune!"

"So you believe that miracles can happen?" I asked, checking to make sure my tape recorder was picking up our voices in the car.

"You're calling them miracles, Liz. I'm not. I believe that if you want something bad enough, you'll do it. You'll be stimulated enough to do it."

"What about—"

"Let me finish, Liz," Bob said. "Your adrenaline will make you do things that nothing else will. In the war, that's been shown a dozen times. Someone will drag a buddy across rocks and mountains. They have a mission. The adrenaline pours out. They can do things that under ordinary circumstances they could never do."

"But what about the people who get out of wheelchairs and stay out of them?"

"That," he said, "you'll have to document."

"I have."

"I'd like to see that."

"Then would you believe that it's not just adrenaline?"

"I'm saying this," Bob said. "Anyone who has faith can move mountains. And that's what we saw tonight."

"Can I quote you on that?" I asked, as John pulled into their driveway.

"That tape deck hasn't been running for no reason," he said, laughing as he got out of the car.

"I'm glad your ribs feel better," I called out the window.

"She's amazing!" he called back.

The day of the next service, Grace phoned. It was late in the afternoon. "Got a pencil?" she asked in a rush. "They're all in the van waiting for me."

The incongruous picture of Grace in a flowing gown, gunning a van along winding Connecticut roads on the way to a service, was a hard one to imagine.

"Sheryl Thompson is going to be at the service tonight," Grace said. "She's bringing her little boy, Ronald."

"Who are they?" I asked.

"Very special people," Grace said. "They've got a truly interesting story."

"You want me to interview them?"

"Yeah. I'll get one of the ushers to point them out," she said.

"What happened?"

"When I prayed over Ronald, his contact lens popped out of his eye. His vision went from twenty/four hundred to twenty/twenty."

"You're talking miracle," I said.

Grace chuckled and said, "God's good."

"Who's going to believe all this stuff?" I asked. I didn't really intend to say that. It just sort of came out as I remembered Bob Madison's reaction. Even with concrete evidence, it's unbelievable.

After interviewing the Thompsons, I pieced their story together in careful detail. In 1980, when Ronald was four years old, his mother had taken him to an ophthalmologist in Clifton, New Jersey. There she learned that her son was blind in one eye. A cataract blocked his vision. He would need surgery.

Sheryl asked to see a specialist. She wanted the finest. He sent her to see a Dr. Warren M. Klein. After several weeks, her son had the operation at the Newark Eye Institute. Following the surgery, he had to wear a contact lens.

Four years later, the cataract reappeared. On March 19, 1984, Ronald was scheduled for another operation. However, that morning the family woke up to a snowstorm. Their car was buried under seven inches of snow. Sheryl's husband went out to clean the snow off the car and shovel the driveway. They had to get an early start; the hospital was two hours away. But when he put the key in the ignition, the battery was dead. It would not start. They had no choice but to postpone the surgery.

The following evening, Sheryl learned that Grace would be in New Jersey, not far from where they lived. The rest of their story matches Grace's. When Grace prayed over the little boy, his contact lens popped out of his eye. His vision cleared.

A month later, I received a doctor's report from Dr. Klein, forwarded to me by Sheryl. It stated that on March 11, 1984, approximately one week before Ronald had seen Grace, his vision was 20/400. On his following check-up, his vision was 20/20 without ever having had surgery or any correction.

It was hard to deny that some sort of miracle was happening. Certain facts, as shown in before-and-after clinical studies by competent specialists, could not be disputed. Further, in the case histories I was able to investigate, coincidence and simple spontaneous re-mission were practically ruled out as causes.

There was also no question in my mind that anyone who carefully observed Grace's services over a length of time would rule out any sort of posing or acting on the part of the afflicted. Their surprise, the intensity of their feeling, their emotional response, their un-qualified testimony, and then of course the lifting of the physical symptoms were genuine beyond any doubt. The sheer quantity of cases—hundreds of them, even thousands—eliminated the possibility of any kind of stage management.

My interviews with twelve-year-old Jeffrey Comeau and eight-year-old Ronald Thompson were even more convincing than those with adults who had been healed. Perhaps it was because their childlike faith allowed them to accept beyond a shadow of a doubt that they had received miracles. I kept thinking about what Jef-frey had said to his mother while they waited for the final lab work: "Mom, I told you Jesus healed me. You always sweat the small stuff."

Ronald, too, had been just as confident about his healing. As he and Sheryl sat in the doctor's examining room several days after they had seen Grace, he turned to his anxious mother and said, "Mom, Jesus made my vision perfect. He didn't want me to lose any more of those expensive contact lenses."

For Jeffrey and Ronald, it was as simple and uncom-plicated as that. For Holly Couture, a six-year-old from Massachusetts, it was so as well.

In 1980, when Holly was in the first grade, a letter was sent home requesting that her vision be checked. A complete eye examination determined that she had amblyopia, a condition creating dimness of vision. Less than a year later, the condition had become severe. The left eye was capable of only finger vision—the ability to discern a finger at a distance of three to four feet. The ophthalmologist suggested that her right eye be patched.

Nine days later, Holly's mother heard about Grace from friends and, desperate to save her daughter's eyesight, took Holly to a service.

"Grace kept calling out for someone to come forward with ear problems," Mrs. Couture recounted during an interview. "Several people got up. But Grace kept saying that there was someone else with ear problems who was still seated. Frankly, I was so worried about Holly's eyes that I had forgotten that she also had constant ear infections and had to have tubes inserted to drain the fluid. It was Holly who said, 'Mommy, she's talking about me.'

"We went up," Mrs. Couture continued. "As Grace put her hands over Holly's ears, I told her that she also had eye problems. I wasn't sure Grace heard me, because her eyes were closed and she looked as if she were deep in prayer. But after she prayed over her ears, she put her hand over Holly's eyes. A few moments later, she asked Holly to cover her right eye, look at the clock at the back of the auditorium, then tell her what time it was.

"When Holly answered her correctly, I nearly fainted. In the past, Holly couldn't even see me with her bad eye if I was only five feet away. Then Grace asked one of the ushers standing way in the back to hold up his fingers for Holly to count. Each time he did it, Holly called out how many he had held up, even though her good eye was covered."

Mrs. Couture ended by saying that the only person more excited than Holly was she herself and that if I would like medical proof, she would ask the doctor to send a letter verifying the facts. A week later, a letter arrived from Dr. Leon Gellerman's office.

When Holly Couture was first seen at our office May 1, 1981, she had experienced severe visual difficulty with her eyes, especially the left eye being that of only finger vision at a distance of three to four feet.

She was then seen by Dr. Botnick, an Ophthalmologist who confirmed that she had severe amblyopia of the left eye and suggested patching the right eye as much as possible.

On attending a healing service approximately nine days later, Grace Di Bicarri, an Evangelist, prayed for Holly.

On June 23, 1981, I re-examined Holly and found that her right eye and left eye both improved to 20/20.

The more doctors' statements I read, the more confused I became. The people being healed were as diverse as their illnesses. If what Dr. Madison said was true— "faith will move mountains"—then I began to wonder what the components of this ethereal "faith" were that would not only move mountains but cure diseased lungs, cataracts, paralysis, deafness, and the like?

In an effort to learn more, I contacted George Meek, an engineer and inventor with scores of successful industrial patents to his credit. What interested me was that he was a pragmatic scientist who had spent the last fifteen years critically observing the activities of healers in the British Isles, Brazil, Europe, South Africa, the Philippines, and the United States.

"You're dealing with something so complex," George Meek said when we met, the morning after he had flown up from his home in North Carolina to see Grace. "In some respects, it's more complicated than the subject of relativity."

"I better warn you," I told George, "my grasp of physics is on the par of a game-show host."

"I'll keep it simple," George said, smiling.

He proceeded to take several pamphlets and half a dozen papers with illustrations out of a natural leather briefcase and spread them out on the kitchen table. Dressed in a pin-striped suit, he looked like a Mobil Oil executive at a board meeting.

"If I speak dogmatically, Liz, it's not because it's George Meek speaking," he said with token humility. "It's because I've had the good fortune to work with roughly a dozen men who are real professionals in medicine, psychiatry, and physics. As a team, we spent several years trying to penetrate the complicated subject of what is going on between healers and their subjects. For me, it was a tremendous pleasure to sit there during Grace's three-hour service. I couldn't help but relate it to the experiences I had studying healers in Brazil and England. But I must say that Grace stands out as one of the high spots of all my contacts in the healing field.

"I'm going to give you several ways to look at what happened last night with Grace and the people from the audience. Now," George said, pointing to an illustrated chart, "what do you know about the placebo effect?"

"A sugar pill used for its psychological effect?" I asked.

"Right," George said. He snapped his briefcase closed and took a sip of coffee. "But this word automatically turns a lot of us off. It implies that all they're doing is kidding themselves with a sugar pill instead of powerful medicine. But what is happening with Grace is a combination of factors that help to create the placebo effect.

"I'll begin with her voice," George said. "It has an impact at a very deep level of a person's soul, psyche. The musical accompaniment is simple. But again, it is a powerful contribution to the placebo effect. The young man singing and playing guitar with direct simplicity is an important part."

"You mean a big orchestra would have destroyed the effect?" I asked.

"Exactly," George said. "And another part of the placebo effect is Grace's incredibly charismatic personality. It speaks to the personality of the people at a very deep level.

"The third factor," George continued, "is crowd action. The group interaction goes on at many levels—all unconscious, as far as the people are concerned. Each one is benefited greatly by the realization that he is one of a group of seekers. They don't think, no matter what their relatives say, that going to see Grace is crazy. So the size of the crowd and the interest of the crowd help to work at a very deep level. There is tremendous camaraderie.

"Another factor is the religious terminology. I speak specifically of such terms as 'the blood of the lamb' and 'Jesus died for you.' These phrases build a bridge between where she is and where the people are. In many cases, Grace is bringing people up in the level of spiritual development by using such terminology.

"Another thing she's doing that is very, very important is to give the disclaimer, 'We're not tied in with any denomination, Catholic, Protestant, Jewish, or the like.' She is simply telling a straightforward message. That in itself is a great contribution to the placebo effect that is being built up.

"Something else high on the list," George continued, "is that she's a superb actress."

"Actress?" I asked. "How do you mean?"

"Now, I want to make it clear," George said, "that when I say she's an actress, I don't mean that she's trying to put on a show for selfish purposes or anything. She's trying to do the best possible job she can of conveying a message to the people. She senses everything that's going on with the person. She does all the right things at the right time."

"And that contributes to the placebo effect too?" I said.

"A very important part." George quickly checked his notes and then went on. "Another thing that is present and is powerful is what I can only loosely call ecstasy. The people's thoughts and emotions are raised to the point where you can just look at their faces and see that they are ecstatic. They're getting something that they've sought all their life. They're so happy to have it. The feeling permeates me as I talk about it.

"To add it all up, these are the factors that are in effect bringing about the changes at the physical level of the person's being. They are at least as effective, and often more effective, than any combination of medicines that a doctor might prescribe. The mind," George said, tapping one of the illustrated charts that depicted the brain, "is being programmed positively. Ultimately, he will wind up in a physical state of health and well being.

"However," George quickly added, pointing to another chart, "if the mind is programmed negatively, and a person has a false assessment of life—for instance, they think that the world is against them and everyone they deal with is a crook—if this happens, the psychiatrists say that you will get into deviating from proper form, and you will wind up in a condition of illness, suffering, and so on.

"We are all immersed in a sea of energy," George said, "and we are intimately connected with that energy. Our cells generate their own electricity. It flows through all the nerves. We know how the energy flows out to all parts of the body." George paused a moment to ask if I knew how many cells made up each human being.

"Millions?" I answered.

"Trillions!" George said. "Sixty trillion cells. And these cells are dying and being replaced at the rate of 5 million cells per second. Let's say a person has cancer. The question is, are those replacement cells going to be duplicates of those crazy cancer cells? Or are they going to be built in the original form?"

"Let me see if I understand this whole thing," I said. "What you're saying is that Grace is putting people into a positive frame of mind through her voice, charisma, compassion, religious terminology, and so forth, so that healings can occur?"

George nodded. He was about to speak, but I stopped him.

"Wait a minute. You're also saying that the healings that happen at her services are all self-healings and are not divinely inspired?"

"I'm saying that Grace is the epitome of what I consider to be a highly developed spiritual being. I am convinced that she is indeed in touch with the universal energy, which, in man's present ignorance of such matters, we can only refer to by such terms as *love, cosmic consciousness, universal mind, the Father,* and *God.*

"But I'm also saying that our years of careful study of healers and the healing process itself have shown that all healing is basically self-healing. Probably less than one percent of mankind can accept this profound truth. Grace is using her God-inspired energy to awaken the undreamed-of self-healing power that God granted to each of us. This self-healing capability is the true 'miracle.' "

"Grace believes indisputably that it is Jesus who is doing the healing," I said.

"Yes. Neither Grace nor any other healer can 'heal.' They are simply the instrument, the conduit. When the Nazarene finished teaching His disciples how He healed the blind, deaf, lame, and demented, He said, 'These things I do, you can do also. Greater things than these can you do.' This applies to every person alive on the planet today. What separates Grace from the mass of humanity is that she has personal courage and superb spiritual attunement with the Nazarene. The result is a remarkable healing service such as I witnessed in Greenwich."

George told me a joke before he left our home to catch his plane back to North Carolina.

"A couple of men at a big corporation had gone to a staff meeting," he said. "They came out and looked at each other, and one fella said to the other, 'Well, I was confused when I went into this meeting. But now I'm confused on a higher level.' " It summed up exactly how I felt.

Shortly after George Meek's erudite and complex explanation, I ran across an illuminating article in *The New York Times*. It pointed out that current scientific thinking demonstrates that our conditioned reflexes make it possible for the brain to exercise direct control over the body's immune defense system; the brain can dispense chemicals that have a direct effect on the immune cells. It occurred to me that if the brain can trigger such an effect, then perhaps an almost magical physical healing can come about simply by having the mind be influenced, or even deeper than the mind, the human soul, which Grace seemed to touch through the divine power she called upon. Here, I was thinking, the rational and the spiritual were brought together in equal parts.

CHAPTER NINE ᪣᪣

I was Christmas Eve, 1982. Nella and William Norbut were doing what they had done every Christmas Eve for the last nine years: They were decorating a tree with delicate Austrian bulbs and handcrafted wooden ornaments and arranging toys for their two sleeping daughters, Michele, nine, and Andrea, four. And finally, they would eat the cookies and drink the milk that had been left next to the fireplace for Santa Claus.

"Everything has to be just perfect," Nella told her husband—he was under the tree trying to get the electric train back onto its track. But everything was far from perfect. He looked up at his wife from beneath the tree. She was placing a Barbie doll into a toy carriage. Her hand was trembling. Her eyes were distant. For the first time, he noticed that her skin was turning yellow.

In November, Nella had been diagnosed as having incurable liver cancer. It had been confirmed by several biopsies and by leading physicians at the University of

Connecticut Health Center. She had been given no more than three months to live.

Nella had left the hospital too weak to return home to take care of her two girls. Too sick even to take care of herself, she and Andrea had moved in with her mother; Michele stayed with her father. In the evenings, William and Michele would come for dinner, then go home to sleep. But after a few weeks of this arrangement, Nella could no longer stand to have the family separated. There was such a short time left. Every moment counted. Within two weeks, William moved out of their house and gave away all their furniture, and he and Michele moved in with his mother-in-law. This brought Nella a certain peace of mind; now she wouldn't have to worry about who would take care of the girls while William worked during the day. Her mother adored the girls—she would be her replacement. With that settled, Nella began to get her personal affairs in order and make the grim arrangements for her own funeral.

The worst time of day was after the girls went to bed. Nella would lie awake haunted by visions of her two girls on the day when she had told them the news.

"Mommy has to go to heaven," Nella told Andrea and Michele one afternoon. She had just returned from the doctor's. The news was worse than ever. The chemotherapy had not shrunk the tumors. "God needs me there," she continued. "But Grandma and Daddy are going to be here for you. They love you as much as Mommy. And they're going to take good care of you." Then she added, "And one day we're all going to be in heaven together."

Four-year-old Andrea didn't understand death. She cried only because Michele and her mother were crying. "And then after you die, Mommy," Andrea asked, "are you going to come back for my birthday party?"

Nella didn't know how to answer her. Some days Nella felt so nauseated from the chemotherapy that she wished her three months were already up. Other days, when she felt a little better, she sat on the sofa and cried until she made herself nauseated.

"Maybe that's what life's all about," Nella told her mother. "My life's been too good. William and I have been truly happy. The kids are healthy. We're a close family. Nothing was wrong with our lives up until this. Maybe this is how you pay for it."

Nella's mother wouldn't listen to her. "The doctors don't know what they're talking about," she said whenever Nella began to talk about dying. "It's just temporary. This time next year, you're going to be back in your own house. You'll be helping me!"

"I wish I could believe that," Nella said, "but look at this skin. I'm yellow as mustard."

Ever since Nella's condition had been diagnosed, her favorite cousin, Gloria, had been trying to persuade her to see a healer she had seen advertised in the local newspaper called Grace 'N Vessels. The ad read, "Come expecting your miracle from God."

"You have nothing to lose," Gloria would say to Nella each time she phoned. But Nella didn't believe in healers. In fact, after she became sick, she had lost faith that there was a God. Gloria, however, was unrelenting. Finally Nella gave in.

Two weeks later, Gloria and Nella arrived at the Crosby High School auditorium in Waterbury, Connecticut, a half-hour late. Grace was already onstage singing. Nella was impressed by her voice and by the fact that practically every seat was taken. She and her cousin found two seats together in the last row. But when the "miracles" began to happen, Nella got suspicious.

"They're plants," Nella said confidently to her cousin.

What bothered Nella as much as the "shills" planted in the audience was that there were so many people stretching their arms to the sky, clapping and praising Jesus.

"We're surrounded by a bunch of fanatics," she whispered to Gloria, adding, "I'm ready to leave if you are."

But Gloria was not ready to leave, not without first getting Nella up for a healing. "We came this far," Gloria said. "You have to at least give it a try." Her voice was firm. She pulled Nella out into the aisle.

Reluctantly, Nella followed her cousin and a procession of others down the aisle to the apron of the stage. Nella watched person after person collapse onto the auditorium floor. Two thoughts ran through her mind: One, this must be some sort of hypnosis. Two, if she went down, her wig might fall off. In the past two months, she had lost all of her hair to the chemotherapy.

When Grace approached Nella, her entire body stiffened. But the instant Grace took hold of her hands, her muscles relaxed. Warmth flowed through her.

"It felt as if someone had poured a warm, soothing liquid through me. Sort of a spiritual chemotherapy," Nella told her cousin on the way home. "In the instant Grace touched me, a powerful peace came over me. I'm almost sure Jesus has healed me. In fact, I *know* it."

That evening was the last time Nella ever took a pain pill, the last time she got nauseated from the chemotherapy or felt sorry for herself. Every week thereafter, Nella attended one of Grace's services. Each time she went into the healing line, that same feeling of a liquid warmth flowed through her. That same

154

"knowing" that Jesus had healed her was indisputably present.

Nella's doctor, Nicholas J. Robert, M.D., then at the University of Connecticut Medical Center, did not share her optimism. Although Nella didn't mention anything about the "miracle healing," she did tell him how great she felt. No longer was there pain or nausea. She even took off her blond wig and showed him that her hair was starting to grow back in spite of the continued chemotherapy. The doctor was glad that she was feeling better, but the facts were on the biopsy slides and on the scans. The cancerous tumors that covered most of her liver were *not* shrinking. In fact, Adrianmycin, the type of chemotherapy she was receiving, had never cured any of his patients. It had merely slowed the cancer's growth temporarily. Simply, no cure rate for her condition had ever been reported medically with Adrianmycin. It would only be a matter of time.

By March, Nella was feeling so good that she no longer wanted to stay around the house. She decided to return to work part-time. Every day when she awoke, she thanked Jesus for her healing. Now she only prayed that very soon the liver scans would show that there was no cancer, enabling her to go off the chemotherapy, which was beginning to show signs of causing cardiac damage.

Because of this side effect of the chemotherapy, Dr. Robert made another decision: In August, he would operate and insert a pump that would deliver the Adrianmycin directly to the liver, alleviating the toll it was taking on her heart and other organs.

The evening before the operation, Nella lay in the hospital bed, her husband at her side. "I don't know why I'm here," Nella said to William, annoyed that the doctors refused to believe that she no longer had the cancer. "Jesus healed me," she told the nurse who had come in to give her a sleeping pill. The nurse politely nodded and left.

William didn't know what to believe. On the one hand, the doctors told him that even with the pump his wife would have only months. On the other hand, Nella appeared to be *anything* but a dying woman. Just the week before, they had been in Disney World in Florida. For three days, Nella ran around the amusement park, sampling all the rides with at least as much gusto as their two small daughters. In the evening, after dinner, it was Nella who insisted that they go back to the park and stay until after the fireworks.

Nella awoke from her surgery the following afternoon. William was at her side.

"Well," she asked her husband, "have they put the pump in?"

William did not answer. He turned to the doctor, who was at the foot of her bed, for an explanation.

"There were *no* tumors," the doctor said, smiling. "The cancer is gone. Biopsies have been taken. Everything is just fine."

In 1984, two years later, Nella supplied me with the before-and-after biopsy reports. It seemed certain to my inexperienced eye that some kind of miracle must have happened, but as a lay person I had no way of interpreting the reports fully. The first report, written before Nella went to Grace's service, read, "Liver biopsies show part scarring with granulomas and part replacement by a malignant neoplasm. The tumor is composed of tightly packed anaplastic cells."

Further down on the page was the comment, "The tumor is undifferentiated. . . . The best bet is an undifferentiated carcinoma, mucin producing with abundant glycogen. With this in mind, renal cell carcinoma and hepatocellular carcinoma are serious considerations." It was dated November 10, 1982.

Nine months later, on August 15, 1983, the new pathology report stated, "Compared to the previous biopsy S82–3163 which demonstrated an infiltrating anaplastic tumor, there is no evidence of malignancy in the present specimen, and numerous sections fail to demonstrate any infiltrates similar to the previous biopsy."

But there was still a question in my mind: Could it have been the chemotherapy that had done the healing? I needed to verify the cure in full detail.

Shortly before I received the biopsy reports, I had been discussing the whole phenomenon of Grace's healing with Dr. Robert Altbaum, a leading internist in Westport, a graduate of the Harvard Medical School, and a physician with a cool sense of objective detachment.

He was curious about the reports he had heard on Grace and indicated that he would like to see her in action, if only to study the phenomenon. I arranged for him and his wife to attend a nearby service. Several days later, I got his reaction. He admitted that he had gone to the service with the intention of trying to figure out the trick. But after sitting in the front row for four hours, after seeing hundreds of people collapse at Grace's touch, including his own pragmatic wife, and after hearing dozens claim instant healings, he left the service completely puzzled.

"If Grace is using some sort of trick to get people to fall down or to say that they're healed," Dr. Altbaum told me, "I don't know what it is. And if it's not a trick, what on earth is she doing at local high schools? She should be seen by millions!" Then he added cautiously, "If she's for real, that is."

Probably the most convincing aspect of the entire service for him had been seeing his wife go over. "I know Lanie," he said. "And she doesn't like to fall under *any* circumstance. Especially for Christian faith healers."

I questioned Lanie Altbaum about what she had felt when Grace laid hands on her. She reported experiencing practically the same sensation as Eleanor Goodrich: For a brief moment, she lost consciousness; this was followed by a completely relaxed, peaceful feeling.

"I've been giving this a lot of thought," Dr. Altbaum said when I ran into him in town two weeks later. "I'm convinced that it's not a trick. But I don't know what the phenomenon is." And then he offered his professional assistance in reviewing any medical reports.

I didn't waste any time getting Nella Norbut's pathology report to him. That same night, my husband and I met Dr. Altbaum and Lanie at an auction at the day-care center that our children attend. In an empty room festooned with infant seats and playpens, he pored over the three-page medical report.

Ten minutes later, he looked up and said, "You know, Liz, this is a very interesting pathology. You have a top-notch medical center and doctor involved."

The medical center he was referring to was the University of Connecticut. Dr. Nicholas J. Robert had recently left Connecticut to assume the position of clinical director of medical oncology at Tufts New England Medical Center in Boston.

"But I'm still suspicious," Dr. Altbaum added. "I wonder if Mrs. Norbut would give me permission to talk directly to Dr. Robert and get the exact details."

He explained that the type of cancer she was diagnosed as having was definitely not curable with Adrianmycin. "Either she didn't have cancer to begin with, or something quite out of the ordinary happened. I'd like to find out."

I told him I was confident that Nella would cooperate, and I was right. Less than one week later, Dr. Altbaum phoned back.

"I finally got in touch with Dr. Robert at Tufts," he said. "Not only did Nella Norbut have a second confirmation, but she had a third." The three biopsies had been done at the University of Connecticut, Duke University, and the American Institute of Pathology.

"They all showed cancer?" I asked.

"Every one of them," he said. "All positive."

"What did Dr. Robert have to say about the case?"

"Well, that it was very bizarre," Dr. Altbaum said. "I told him that she had gone to see a faith healer."

"And?"

"He more or less couched it."

"What does that mean?" I asked.

"He said that there was no way he was going to stand up in front of a conference of oncologists and say that one of his patients had been cured by a faith healer. But he also said that he wouldn't stand up and say that Adrianmycin cured one of his patients either."

"What do you think?"

"I think that you have a watertight case," Dr. Altbaum said. "It's well documented. You're dealing with highly respected doctors, first-rate medical centers, before-and-after biopsies. You can't get better than that."

For every dramatic physical healing like Nella Norbut's, there seemed to be dozens of psychological ones for those with addictions and for the emotionally disturbed. Early on in my research, Dorothy, one of Grace's ushers, came to me and said, "Liz, whatever you do, don't ignore all of us who have been helped psychologically. You can live with being crippled and blind. But you can't live if you're severely depressed or an addict."

I recalled two vivid and dramatic scenes that I had observed at two of Grace's services. In the first, which took place in a Greenwich school auditorium, Grace came down to the area in front of the stage apron and said, "The Lord tells me that there are at least a dozen or two here tonight who are actively thinking of committing suicide. I know what terrible agony is boiling inside of you. I know how you must be craving release from this terrible urge. And I know what you must do about it at once, before it's too late."

She paused and her eyes flashed around the audience in front of her. Then she added, "I also know how painful it might be for you to come forward in front of your friends, your families and the hundreds of people here tonight, to accept a miracle—a miracle that you must have in order to change your life—to go on living, to receive a sense of self-worth.

"I am now asking you to do this very thing. To come up here in spite of embarrassment and fear. To relieve yourself of the burden that is bearing down on you. Maybe you don't believe that there is a God. Well, come on down anyway and find out."

Grace paused again. No one from the audience stirred. I remembered feeling an overwhelming sense of both hope and despair for those people, whoever they might be. But I also felt that in such a circumstance, I myself would never have the strength to go forward openly in front of so many people and reveal my inner compulsion. The physical healings were one thing, but revealing the thought of taking one's own life was another.

There was still no movement in the audience; still no one dared to come forward under such a challenge. After another pause, Grace said, "God is waiting for you to come up here. He is opening His arms to give you strength and courage. Please don't wait. Please come."

I turned and looked back over the sea of faces in the audience. There was a deathly silence throughout the auditorium. Then I saw one man several rows behind me rise hesitantly. He was dressed in a business suit with a regimental striped tie; his hair was groomed, his expression impassive. He moved across several seats in his row and came down to the edge of the stage. My heart went out to him. Then suddenly a woman in the back of the auditorium also rose. Her face was strained, her eyes vacant, her steps uncertain as she made her way forward. By the time these first two had reached the edge of the stage, half a dozen others joined the procession toward Grace, and within minutes there were some twenty people lined up in a row across the front of the audience, standing expressionless. It was a scene I couldn't believe and can never forget.

Grace moved across the line, touching them lightly on their foreheads, blessing them as she did so. Some of them toppled backward; others staggered back a few steps. By the time she had moved across the line, over a dozen of them were unconscious on the floor. My thoughts raced. This had to be the ultimate tribute to Grace and her service—an open public confession— and with it a release from one of the most devastating impulses a person could face.

An equally moving scene took place at a Danbury service when Grace asked all who would admit to drug addiction and alcoholism to come forward. Again, I found it hard to believe that anyone would accept such a challenge in front of friends and family. To admit such a weakness in the glaring public eye would be too much to expect. But as before, at least two dozen came forward, many of them young people in their teens and twenties.

This had happened many times before, I learned later. The story Dorothy told me was only one of hundreds of such cases. Like her fellow usher, Al, Dorothy had been addicted to both drugs and alcohol. However, in Dorothy's case, neither she nor her husband had realized it until after the healing had taken place.

"The only time I went to church was to baptize my children," the pert-faced blonde said as we sat in Grace's Greenwich office. "So I'm sitting in this church that my in-laws took us to, and Grace is only about a half an hour into the service. My husband is trying to figure out if she's hypnotizing people. And Grace is looking up and down the aisle in our row and the next. She looked at my husband and then at my children. And she stopped at me. All she did was look at me, and I began to squirm in my seat. But she was looking at me as if she could see right through me.

"In the church, Grace continued to look at me for a long time, and she nodded her head and said to my husband, 'She has a nice smile.' Then she motioned for me to get up in front of everybody. I whispered to my husband, 'I don't believe this.' But I didn't want to argue with her. I got up feeling silly. I made my way around to the front, where she was. I said to myself that I felt sorry for this lady so I don't want to embarrass her. I said to her that I was not going to fall over. I was thinking to myself that I'm not the hysterical type, I'm an educated businesswoman, and there's absolutely nothing wrong with me. Sometimes I might drink too much and smoke too much grass, but I'm certainly not addicted. Later, I realized that this was all part of the addict's denial.

"The next thing I knew, she anointed me with oil and touched my forehead. At that point I felt a breath of fresh air that lifted me up and laid me down. I was conscious, but I couldn't move: I couldn't move my legs. I couldn't move my arms. Then I felt everything centered on my heart. I felt as if someone had my heart in his hand. My heart was rolling in my chest. I thought I was having a heart attack. I thought I was going to die. It was just rumbling in my chest. It was deafening my ears. I must be having a heart attack, I kept saying. But that's okay. I felt relaxed. I said, 'Oh my God, I think I'm going to die,' but yet I was at peace. It was the most unreal thing I ever felt. The next thing I knew, I could move first one foot, then the other. I quickly got to my feet and ran back to my chair."

Dorothy had to break off at this point to answer the phone at the desk. Grace's regular volunteer was sick.

"When I walked out of that place," Dorothy continued, "I thought I was the same girl. But the very next day, I walked into the kitchen to pour a cup of coffee and I heard an audible voice say, 'You'll never be sick again.'

"When I heard that voice, it was as if someone came over and spoke to me. I can't describe it. I know it was God, because a peace had come over me that I had never known before.

"That night, I did what I did every other night—I poured myself a huge goblet of wine. But when I took my first sip, it didn't taste the same. I took a few more sips. Each sip got worse. I ended up dumping it into the sink. The next couple of days, the exact same thing happened.

"That weekend my husband and I went to a wedding. Someone lit up a joint and passed it around. I went to take it, but then something stopped me. It was as if I couldn't physically reach out my arm. Within one week, my life had turned right around. And I said, 'Oh my God, something has really happened. I need someone to talk to.' I had a joy and peace like you couldn't imagine.

"I called up the prayer line and said that I really had to talk to somebody because my life had changed. Something had really happened to me, and I didn't know what it was. The person on the other end of the line said, 'You mean you didn't need anything in your life?' And I said, 'Well, I didn't think anything was wrong with me.' And she said that she would like me to call and make an appointment to see Grace. And you see, Liz," Dorothy said, "here I am today."

While Dorothy was relating her story, Esther Porricelli had come into the office. The trim, attractive woman in her late fifties bent down to the sofa and gave each of us a warm hug hello. Then she blew a kiss over to Grace, who was at her desk opposite us. Grace was counseling a young man dressed in jeans and a T-shirt.

"I thought you kids might want a snack," Esther said, softly so as not to disturb Grace. She was carrying a huge pastry box, overflowing with Italian cookies and tiny iced cakes. "Joe just took these out of the oven," Esther said with the same pride as if she had personally baked them. Esther was referring to the baker in the supermarket downstairs, one of the Food Marts she and her husband owned. It was because of the Porricellis that Grace had the large oak-paneled office in the chic Greenwich shopping district. They had donated it to the ministry because they believed in what Grace was doing.

And they had good reason. Esther had had her own miracle. Anyone looking at her today, with her ever-present smile and bouncy step, would find it hard to believe that only two years earlier she had been so deeply depressed that she was unable to function.

"For the last thirty-five years," Jerry Porricelli, the wealthy Greenwich businessman, said as he sat down on the sofa to join us, "I watched my wife sink lower and lower. I was scared, because every day was worse than the day before. When I went to the office in the morning, I didn't know what I'd find when I came home. Usually I would have to go home several times a day to check on her. And the worst part about all of this is that we're financially able to get the best medical treatment. But even the finest psychiatrists could not help." Jerry brushed his thick sandy-gray hair back.

"Here I had my two beautiful sons, grandchildren, house, and everything else," Esther said, "and I couldn't enjoy anything. Some days I was too frightened to get out of bed. Forget about leaving the house—for thirty-five years, I was not alive."

"The night I went to see Grace," Jerry continued the story, "I went alone. At that point, Esther rarely left the house. I was standing in the back, and something just told me that here was a woman who could help my wife."

The evening Grace came to their home, four days later, marked the beginning of a new life for both of them. "I had never seen anyone so despondent," Grace, who had finished counseling the young man, recalled. "I walked into this huge mansion-type house. There, lying on the sofa, was a woman. I thought at first she was dead. She wasn't moving. She was just lying there. Sort of shrunken."

"I don't think I weighed a hundred pounds," Esther added. She was nibbling on a piece of cake.

"I went over to her," Grace said, "and I told her that we were going to pray for her depression to leave."

"I knew something was happening to me," Esther said. "It was as if I was lying on the sofa with fifty-pound weights on top of me. And as we prayed, I felt the weights becoming lighter and lighter."

"God showed me that her depression was lifting," Grace said. She clutched Esther's hand as she remembered that evening. "God was coming into her life and filling her with His love and joy. He doesn't want anyone to suffer."

"I can't even remember hugging my two sons as they were growing up," Esther said. But there didn't seem to be regret in her eyes or voice. She was now making up for it, she said. "I don't waste time thinking about the past. I've got too much to live for right now. Jesus came into my heart and taught me how to live and love again. And that's what I'm doing, every single day."

"The first thing Esther and I do in the morning," Jerry said, "is to thank the good Lord for giving us a beautiful day and a life we're happy to live."

"I feel that's a miracle, don't you?" Esther said as she gave my hand a squeeze. "Come on, Liz, I want to introduce you to our friends who work downstairs in the store. We'll get you some cookies to take home to your little boy." As we headed out the door, she added, "Enough talk about the *old* Esther."

It was Grace herself who suggested I talk with William Hampton, M.D., chief of psychiatry at Greenwich Hospital. I hoped that as a psychiatrist, he could throw some light on the methods Grace used from a scientific point of view.

I was surprised to learn not only that Dr. Hampton was referring patients to Grace but also that he had even invited Grace to his home, where she conducted private healing sessions.

"We might not understand Grace in terms of scientific explanations," Dr. Hampton told me during a phone interview. "But we know that this type of healing does exist. Most physicians use a form of this unknowingly. We can't explain everything. But just because we can't explain what Grace is doing doesn't mean that it doesn't exist."

"Grace mentioned that you occasionally send some of your patients to her?" I asked.

"Yes," Dr. Hampton said without a moment's hesitation, "I do."

"Have the results been favorable?"

"Yes. It increases their faith. It makes them more willing to help themselves. Their general well-being improves."

I told Dr. Hampton that what surprised me the most was the success that Grace has had with hard-core alcoholics and drug abusers, and the fact that so many experienced instantaneous healings without any withdrawal symptoms. He said that he had personally not seen that happen; the patients he sent to Grace had gone for emotional reasons rather than addictive ones. However, he did have a theory about how that could happen.

"Perhaps the reason why they do experience healings from drugs and alcohol is because they feel inspired,"

Dr. Hampton began. "They suddenly have a deeper purpose—not just wanting to please Mom or Dad. It gives them motivation that no doctor can. Most drug rehabilitation centers and Alcoholics Anonymous have a religious side to them, turning it over to a higher power."

Dr. Hampton went on to say that no one really knows the cause of addiction; therefore it is necessary to rely on more inspirational kinds of work. "Curing the mind is as important as curing the lungs," he added.

When he said *lungs*, I started to tell him about Anthony DeBernardi, the man who had been healed from lung cancer. But before I could finish, he cut in and said, "I respect her work. I don't have to be convinced that people are getting healed. I don't have a great need for explanation. I think scientific explanation has become a modern fad. Everyone needs a scientific answer. I think that this kind of work should stand by itself. If the pain goes away, that's great. But if someone psychologically feels better—that's the answer. We don't need lab tests. I hope you point in that direction. It's what happens in the individual: Is their life enriched? Do they feel better about themselves? Is their general life better? That's the acid test."

Scene after scene unfolded over the long months as I watched Grace apparently bring about endless miracles. Although all the scenes had a sameness, each individual case was unique. Highlights stood out in my mind: a crippled nun who burst into tears when she walked for the first time in years; a thirty-year-old woman with dyslexia who could suddenly read; a seventy-year-old stroke victim who left his walker to run up the aisle; two Catholic priests and the bishop of a large New York parish who stood alongside Grace, hands clasped, arms stretched high in the air, one of them announcing loud and clear, "I have seen Jesus come alive! He is here tonight!"

For me, however, the most intense scene took place not in a church or high school auditorium but in a maximum security prison for women in Bedford Hills, New York.

The day Grace phoned me to say that she had been invited to do a prison service, I asked of her only one favor: That she take along a tape recorder. I wanted to have a clear idea of what it was like. She quickly informed me that that would not be necessary. I would be going along. My name had already been given to the prison officials as one of the Vessels of the ministry.

"Hope you don't mind, Liz," Grace said. "It was the only way I could get you in."

It would give me a great opportunity to see how a large group of people who had never seen her before reacted, she told me. Then when she began to give me details, her enthusiasm bubbled over. I'm sure it never even crossed Grace's mind that I might have second thoughts about going, especially as one of the Vessels.

"We'll all meet at my house at three-thirty. Then we'll hop in the van. And, oh yeah," Grace suddenly blurted out as if she had just remembered it, "I put down Lance's name on the prison list as one of the Vessels too."

Grace was referring to Lance Ballou, a film producer who had been working with us for the last few months on a film possibility. As Grace continued to give further instructions, vivid images flashed before my eyes. I had an incongruous image of Lance dressed in a preppy navy blue blazer and plaid slacks scurrying around the prison auditorium catching the inmates as they toppled into his arms. I also conjured up the image of myself piously holding the jar of anointing oil for Grace. Or maybe, I thought, she would want me to drop the red square swatches of cloth over the prisoners' exposed legs after they landed on the floor. There were always one or two female ushers who performed that function at every service.

The day of the event, I drove up to Grace's house with Alan Bleiman, a lawyer and close friend of hers. He too was going along as one of the Vessels. Alan was an active member of the ministry. Several months earlier, he had accepted Christ as his personal savior, even though he himself was Jewish. When I questioned him about how he combined the two religions, he told me that he didn't think there was any conflict between his Jewish beliefs and his acceptance of Jesus Christ as the Messiah.

"Except for Luke, in the first years of Jesus's ministry all the disciples were Jewish," the thirty-eight-year old lawyer said.

During our forty-five-minute drive up to Grace's in Brookfield, Alan recalled for me the story of how he had gone to see Grace for the first time. He stood in the healing line, and by the time he had returned to his seat, he had accepted Jesus as the Messiah.

"My life was good before," he said straightforwardly. "But now it's even better. I have peace and personal satisfaction that were previously unknown to me."

We pulled into Grace's driveway promptly at three-thirty. It was no great surprise that she wasn't ready. Wearing a bright blue chiffon gown and tearing rollers out of her hair, she darted out of the bedroom to kiss us a quick hello and say that Lance had just phoned. He was on his way.

"Pop a snack into the microwave," Grace told Alan, who was already in the kitchen pouring himself a cup of coffee.

Then she ran back toward her room. I was at her heels, asking for the hundredth time if she was sure I should be going along. Without answering, she pointed toward a king-size bed, smothered with satin pillows in assorted shapes, and told me to have a seat. While she brushed out her hair, I glanced around the room. It looked like a warehouse for dolls. Stacked in the corner were eleven boxes of them. When Grace noticed me staring in disbelief, she said, "I keep those for some of the kids who come to the services. The ones who can't afford toys."

"And the stuffed animals in the other corner too?" I asked.

"Yep," Grace said. She was on the floor of her closet digging for shoes to match her gown. "Those go to the orphanage next week."

"You really care about people," I said, not intending to say that.

"We all care, Liz," Grace said.

"But you seem to care and feel much more than—"

"That's not true," Grace interrupted. "God made each and every one of us to care and to feel for our brothers and sisters. He didn't create me any more sensitive than the next person. When we accept Jesus Christ into our lives, we are able to release our true nature. The goodness in us flows forth. You can't stop it. It just bursts through like a rushing river." She slipped on her shoes and grabbed an oversize leather bag. "We'd better go. You'll see what I'm talking about tonight."

She flipped off the light switch and added, "God loves the women we're going to see in that prison as much as He loves anyone. And their potential for goodness and love is as great as anyone's."

When we arrived on the prison grounds, we were informed by a guard toting a rifle that Grace's service had been moved from six o'clock to seven. Therefore, we would not be allowed to clear security for an hour. We could wait either in our van or in a stark trailer, without chairs or heat, parked next to the guardhouse. We chose to remain in the van. The quarters were cramped, but we were a lively, congenial bunch. In the back with me were Mike, the sound man and one of the Vessels; Alan, Lance, and three regulars, Mary, Brenda, and Patty. Grace was in the driver's seat. Larry was next to her. Moments after she parked the van, they began to pray.

"Lord, touch them, Father," Grace said softly. "We love you and want you to come into the prison through us."

"Yes, Father," Larry said. "We ask you to open doors for us. Free their souls from those prison bars."

Everyone joined in their prayers except for Lance and me. Occasionally, I pulled back the curtain of the van window and peered out. Several large brick buildings sat on top of a rolling hill. Surrounding them were high electrical fences with huge hoops of razor wire coiled around the top. The rain and the blowing wind made the sight even more ominous.

"Heal their hearts along with their physical bodies," Grace continued. Her hand dropped to the steering wheel. Her eyes were shut tightly. "Deliver them, oh Lord, from their sorrow. Let Larry James and I turn our music into one harmony for your healing love."

"Yes, Lord," Larry said. He placed his hand lightly on top of Grace's head. "Let Grace be the tool to go into there tonight and free them. Whoever the Son sets free is free indeed."

"Liz," Lance whispered, "what did Grace mean when she said that I would have to be a 'catcher'?"

I told him he wouldn't have to do it now because Mike was there. Lance appeared to be relieved. He said he was glad for that, because he had a bad back.

Grace must have heard us talking. She turned and said that since we were going in as part of the Vessels, we would have to sing, and it would really help if we prayed too.

"These women are going to need all the prayers they can get," Grace reminded us. Then she asked us all to hold hands, and we began to pray.

"Dear Lord, we come here tonight with love in our hearts for our brothers and sisters. If our life situations had been different, it could be any one of us in there. But you spared us, dear Lord—"

When Grace said those words, something inside of me clicked. What she said was true. Thinking of the prisoners—many of them lifers—we were about to face, I thought of the famous phrase of Oliver Wendell Holmes, who said to a friend as he passed a derelict in a doorway, "There but for the grace of God go I."

We entered the prison through a barred gate. Once we were in the prison auditorium, Grace appeared to be as at home as she had been several weeks earlier at a service at the Maryknoll Convent. Unlike the nuns, however, there was no initial joy on the prison women's faces. Two by two, they entered from behind a large gate. Dressed in prison-green slacks, jumpers, and skirts, they showed little or no emotion as they took their seats. Most watched with vacant stares while Mike and Larry quickly set up a minimal sound system. Some slouched half off their seats, making it pretty obvious, I thought, that probably the only reason they were there was to have an hour away from their cells. Two large women who had the appearance of Sunday School teachers sat in the front row. Their legs were crossed properly at the ankles, and their hands were folded on top of their laps. They too had no expression. Later, I learned that both women were serving life sentences for murder.

Several dozen women stood behind a closed gate, waiting for the first group to be seated before they would be allowed to enter. One young woman with a man's haircut occasionally rattled the gate and shouted, "Hey, Mama, let's get it on!"

Grace, undaunted by the blank faces, began the service by singing her most upbeat song, "I've Got the Faith." Only the Vessels and a handful of prisoners clapped along. When Grace finished the song, she walked to the front row, sensing their feelings, and said, "You might be sitting there saying, 'Sure, it's easy to have her faith. She's free. She didn't grow up with no money, no food, no clothes. With a father who left her, with a father who beat her.' Well, if you're thinking that, you're wrong. Dead wrong." Grace looked as if she were forcibly trying to make eye contact with each woman there as she went on to relate a few of the more gruesome events of her childhood.

"But I didn't go into drugs, prostitution, or stealing," Grace said, dropping her voice, "not because I'm any better than you, but because, at five years old, Jesus came into my life. And *He* saved me! And that is the *only* reason I'm not in here."

Within ten minutes, Grace had become like a magnet for the group. All eyes were drawn to her. Some brimmed with tears; fixed jaws softened. The two women in the front row wiped their eyes.

"The real freedom is not out there," Grace said, pointing to a window with bars, "it's in here. In our heart. Jesus can lift those prison bars from you. *He* can set you free!"

"Yeah, Mama?" the woman with the man's haircut shouted. "Have him get us out of here!"

Grace ignored the outburst. "You're in here saying, 'If only I could do my life over again.' Well, I've got news for you. Right now, you can end those nightmares, those tears. You can become a new person in Jesus Christ. He doesn't care what you've done or said in the past. He loves you *just the way you are!*"

There was a scattering of applause. Grace was breaking through the barrier, and she knew it.

"I came here tonight," Grace continued, "because God said, 'Go tell them about me. Go tell them that I love them just the way they are.' There isn't a person here who has to go back to that room empty. There's a way you can live with peace of mind. Take your burdens to the Lord. He'll lift them from you." Grace walked down the center aisle, her arm extended and her palm turned upward as if to demonstrate graphically that the burden could be lifted.

"If you're good enough for God, you're good enough for anybody!" Grace added.

Again, there was applause. But this time, almost everyone was clapping. Most of the women had also risen from their seats.

"Are you ready to become that new creature in God?" Grace asked. She backed away from the front row, making enough room for the group to come toward her. Then she turned to Larry and cued a song.

By the time Grace had finished singing "I'm Walking With a Man Heading for a Mansion," three-fourths of the group were standing before her.

"Anyone still seated who wants to become a new creature in Christ Jesus," Grace said, "please come forward now."

A few more got up from their seats. Three women in the last row walked slowly forward holding hands. The woman on the end was limping. Her foot looked as if it were deformed. The last person to get up was the woman with the man's haircut. She swaggered forward mumbling, "I'm comin,' Mama—just hang on."

"God's going to break the chains that bind you inside," Grace began. "He's going to set you free right now. Put one hand on your heart. And one up to God. Ask Jesus right now to come into your heart. Say with me, 'Jesus, come into my heart and forgive me of everything I've ever done. Anything I've ever said. I'm sorry, Lord—'" Grace suddenly stopped the prayer. A young woman was sobbing out of control. Grace placed her arms around the woman and gently pulled her close, as if consoling a small child who had just fallen and scraped both knees.

"Jesus is taking that pain from you," she whispered. The woman buried her face in Grace's shoulder. Two male correction officers moved in. Later, I learned why: It was not unusual for some of the women to carry filed-down dinner knives.

"You can't anticipate what some of them are going to do," one guard told me after the service. "I came here from Attica two months ago, and I'm transferring back. Almost every officer in here has a transfer out. It's worse than any man's prison."

"He set you free!" Grace announced to the group at the end of the prayer. "He's going to give each and every one of you peace for the first time in your life. You'll be able to sleep. You'll be able to wake up feeling as if it's a new day, even though you have to stay in prison. You're free!"

Gradually, smiles began to form and hands began to clap as Grace belted out "Jesus Set Me Free."

After the women returned to their seats, Grace walked up and down the aisles, calling out the names of the various ailments she could sense around her.

"I'm not going to say that anyone here has had depression. That has been everyone's problem," Grace said. "But Jesus *has* just lifted that from you. Those who haven't accepted Jesus Christ into your hearts, don't worry. The Vessels and myself will pray that you do."

When Grace said that, I looked over at Lance for his reaction. "What do you think?" I asked.

"I'm amazed," he said. "When we first walked in here, I never thought even *one* of them would crack. They looked like a bunch of tough cookies."

Lance was right. When I first saw the rows of stony faces, I thought that the only miracle would be if we got out alive. But Grace's ability to relate to everyone, from the country club set in Greenwich to the inmates at a maximum security prison, was in itself miraculous. Moments before Grace walked onto the stage, I had whispered to her that I didn't expect everyone to look so angry. Grace, sensing my uneasiness, wrapped one arm around my shoulder and said, "Liz, we're not at a Tupperware party." Then her smile faded, and she added, "They've had a tough life. We're here to show them God's love."

If Grace was nervous, she didn't show it. The only

emotions she displayed were love and compassion as she moved up and down the aisles making physical and spiritual contact with practically every person there while the security guards watched in apprehension.

"Honey," Grace said, pointing to a woman with a deformed foot who minutes earlier had come up to accept Jesus, "we're going to ask God to fix that foot." She placed her hand on top of the foot and prayed aloud.

The woman began to roll her foot around inside an oversize sneaker. The side of the sneaker was practically worn through from walking on it.

"Take it off, honey," Grace commanded.

The large woman slipped it off.

"Now try walking," Grace said.

There were gasps in the audience. The toes that had been curled under, as if from arthritis, began to straighten. The foot that had been resting on its side suddenly looked normal.

"Mama, that's some *baaaad* Jesus!" the woman with the man's haircut mumbled.

"That's right. He's some *baaaad* Jesus," Grace said, speaking the woman's language. "And Jesus is going to fix your heart just like He fixed her foot."

"Okay, Mama, I'm ready."

During the hour-and-a-half service, several cases of arthritis were reported to have disappeared. Two women, both of whom claimed to be totally deaf in one ear, could suddenly hear. One woman said that a lump on her arm just "melted away" as Grace prayed over her. Another said that her blurred vision was gone. Still another said that Jesus took away her migraine headache as she was giving her life to Him.

But none was as poignant as a small, young woman in sunglasses who came over to Grace at the end of the service. "Sister Grace," she said, "this morning my baby daughter was buried. After the funeral, I came back here just tryin' to figure a way to do myself in. But something happened tonight. When you touched me, I felt the power of Jesus come into my whole body. He took away the hate for the man who killed her. And He took the pain away."

As the woman mentioned that her parole would not come up for fifteen years, Grace took her in her arms and said, "From tonight on, Jesus is going to teach you how to live happily and peacefully!"

Seconds later, a guard approached. He indicated with a shift of his eyes that it was time for us to leave. Grace kissed the top of the woman's head. Then we walked back out the same barred gate we had entered.

"You see," Grace said with tears in her eyes, "I'm not as strong as you might have thought."

Grace was no stranger to violence. She once stopped a fight in the streets of Washington, D.C.

"It was around three in the morning," Grace said. "Larry, Mike, and I were returning from the National Christian Broadcasting Convention to our hotel. We were lost. The streets were empty. Everything was closed. There was no one around to ask directions. Suddenly I heard a woman screaming. Then I saw what was happening. She was getting beat up by a man.

"I yelled to Larry to stop the car. He asked me if I was crazy—we should call the police, he said.

"About a block down from where the guy was beating her up, I saw a bar. I figured there would be a telephone in there. Before Larry had a chance to even park the car, I jumped out. There was a long flight of stairs up to the bar. As I was going up, I passed a few of what I thought were women coming down. They were all dressed like they were going to a ball. At the top of the stairs was the bouncer. 'Hi, Butch,' he said to me. 'Welcome to Drag Queen Night. Two pink ladies for the price of one.'

"He had a moustache and a skintight lavender dress on. I explained that down the road a woman was getting beat up and I just wanted to call the police.

"After I called the cops, I passed by the bar. Almost everyone was on the dance floor. It looked like prom night. The music was blasting. I stood on the barstool to get their attention and shouted for some of them to come and help. I figured that there would be safety in numbers. After a few more pleas for help, three big guys said that they would come. I'll never forget the look on Larry's and Mike's faces when they saw me coming out with three guys in dresses. We all took off down the street toward the fight.

"I screamed at the man to let her alone. He was trying to pull her off the sidewalk into the road. The guy just screamed back for us to go away. Larry and Mike were standing on either side of me. The three guys from the bar were circling the couple, ready to hold him back from hurting her anymore. She was lying on the ground, crying. I reached into my purse and took out a wad of Kleenex and wiped her mouth. It looked as if he had knocked out some of her teeth. There was blood all over. One of the guys took off his shawl and placed it under her head as a cushion.

"She seemed to be hurt badly. I told Larry to go back to the bar and call an ambulance. But then she got to her feet. She said that she was okay and that we should just leave them alone. I reminded her that the man had just beat her up. But the man spoke up and said, 'That's okay. She's my wife.'

"Can you imagine, Liz?" Grace continued. "He was mad because we were butting into his business. I just took the girl's arm and said, 'Come on, honey, you're coming with us.'

"The girl was too frightened to leave him. He was threatening that if she went with us, he would kill her when she returned home. It was then that I yelled that he was never going to lay a hand on her again. That God was going to see to that. I told them that God loved them. That He was going to come into their lives right then and there. They were standing there looking at me like I was a crazy nut off the street. But I kept it up. I kept telling them that once they have God in their lives, the fights, hatred, jealousy will leave. Then I told everyone, even the boys from the bar, that we were going to hold hands and pray for that couple. We were all standing in one big circle on the sidewalk of a deserted Washingon, D.C., street, praying. When we finished, the couple held each other and cried openly to be forgiven.

" 'I don't know who you are, lady,' the man said, 'or where you came from, but you just changed our lives.'

"I told him that I didn't change a thing. It was God. He wanted them to know His healing love.

"The three guys from the bar were really spaced out over the whole thing. They walked away shaking their heads, not saying a word. And the police never showed up. But I believe that that was a miracle. If they had come, there would have been an arrest. It just goes to show you—God is the greatest policeman in the world."

CHAPTER TEN 👑👑

"I ALWAYS BELIEVED IN MIRACLES," ANTHONY Estatico, an articulate young engineer told me during an interview. Then he promptly qualified his statement. "For others, that is. I never thought one would happen for me."

Shortly after Anthony graduated from Manhattan College in New York and began his career as a civil engineer, he was diagnosed as having multiple sclerosis, a chronic disease of the central nervous system that most often results in muscular atrophy and permanent invalidism. Within four years of first being diagnosed, Anthony's condition had progressed to the point where he had difficulty standing and walking unassisted. In addition, his hearing and vision were deteriorating rapidly.

"It was actually my brother who suggested I see Grace," Anthony said. "I was in such bad shape that I said, 'Okay, what do I have to lose?' I was on so much medication, and the medication wasn't even working, just causing side effects. I stopped working full-time. I began going to the office only two half-days a week.

Some weeks I didn't go in at all. I just lay in bed, too weak and disoriented to even get up.

"The afternoon before my brother took me to Grace's service, I remember lying flat in bed. I asked the Lord if I should go. My answer was a sudden jolt of energy. I was able to get out of bed and dressed.

"I went up for the altar call—the part of the service where you're expected to invite Jesus Christ into your life," Anthony explained. "Grace placed her hand on the top of my head, and out I went. I didn't feel too much at that point. But later I got into the prayer line. When she touched my forehead, I went out again. This time, I felt a tingling sensation. It lasted for several hours. All my extremities were buzzing."

Anthony stopped his narrative long enough to explain that his was a progressive healing that occurred over a three-month span.

"The next time I went to a service, I was standing in the prayer line and the woman behind me started applauding after someone had been healed. When she did, I felt a twinge in my left ear. Suddenly everything got louder. I got in front of Grace, and when she prayed over me I felt the same thing happen in my right ear.

"But my complete healing took place on August 31 in Greenwich, Connecticut. I went to a service with my mother. When Grace laid hands on me, I not only felt a tingling sensation but I got very, very dizzy. For twenty minutes, or maybe longer, I sat at my seat light-headed. Things were happening throughout my entire body. I could just feel a cleansing going on. It was as if all my symptoms began to disappear. They were lifting. The stiffness and soreness in my legs were gone, right there at the service.

"I turned to my mother," Anthony said, "and told her that I was sure I was now completely healed. I could tell she didn't quite buy the whole thing. Not that she wasn't happy for me, but I could just sense that she was still skeptical.

"Less than a month later, I went back to my doctor. I knew that I was healed, but I just wanted to have the medical proof, probably something to do with my engineering mind." He chuckled. "And this is what really knocked me over: The doctor insisted on repeating the tests *three* times before he could believe the results. 'I don't believe it. I can't find anything wrong with you,' he said.

"All my reflexes were perfectly symmetrical. The doctor said that if he hadn't personally examined me only two months earlier, he would never believe that I had multiple sclerosis. On my previous visit, the MS had spread to my back.

"Before I left his office, I told him that I had been seeking prayer and that the Lord had healed me. At the time I told him that, he confided that as a physician he had seen too many miraculous things happen to doubt the existence of God. But when he sent his statement confirming that I no longer had MS, he was much more circumspect."

Anthony Estatico was examined on 10/16/84. The patient carried the diagnosis of multiple sclerosis. When examined on the above date, there appeared to be no neurological deficit. This would constitute an overall improvement. It is my belief that the improvement is directly related to a "remission" in a patient with multiple sclerosis.

Sincerely yours,
Stephen C. Klass, M.D.

This type of medical statement was the rule in cases Grace was involved in. Only a handful of the physicians I spoke to admitted the possibility of divine healing. Throughout this research, I had to keep reminding myself of what Dr. Kurien had said months earlier: "We can simply say that something has happened here that we do not understand. Those who are religious, such as this woman Grace, may say that a miracle has happened. But I feel that we should simply accept the fact that someone gets better. To me, my goal is that the patient should be well."

It certainly looked that way for Anthony Estatico. Three months after Grace first laid hands on him, he had gone from being totally bedridden to working full-time and resuming an active social life that included outdoor sports. What was also interesting about Anthony's healing was that it was one that developed over several encounters with Grace.

"If Jesus heals you instantly, that's great," Grace tells the audience at almost every service. "But it's just as great if you're healed in stages. Some of you may be healed as you drive home, some as you sleep, some as you work. And then there are some who don't even have to come to a service to be healed.

"Not long ago a woman got in the prayer line holding her husband's handkerchief," Grace said during a service in Greenwich. "The moment I touched that piece of cloth, Jesus showed me that her husband was an alcoholic. After I prayed, I told the lady that her husband would never touch another drink. At that very moment, her husband was home watching TV. He had just opened up another can of beer. But before it reached his lips, the can got so hot he had to drop it. He thought that he was flipping out. He went over and picked it up. The taste was horrible. He never touched another drink after that."

The evening Grace told that story at the Greenwich service, Georgia Mathews was in the audience. She was a forty-five-year-old mother and secretary from Yonkers who had had her own miraculous healing through Grace. Now, two years later, she was back again. This time, she was counting on another miracle, not for herself, but for her daughter Laurie, who was suffering from large pelvic tumors and was unable to be present at the service.

The moment Grace asked if there were any people who wanted special prayer for those who couldn't be there, Georgia rose along with scores of others. Clutched in her hand was a photograph of her daughter. As she waited her turn, Georgia thought back to the first time she had come to see Grace, for her own healing.

It had all been like a dream for Georgia Mathews. Grace had pointed directly at her and said, "You, sister. You have three ruptured discs and sciatica nerve damage." Georgia could hardly believe her ears: How did Grace—a woman who had never laid eyes on her— correctly diagnose her condition?

Georgia's medical prognosis, as certified on her doctor's insurance report, flatly stated that the patient was totally disabled, that she was unable to walk without assistance, and that she was incapable of even sedentary activity. The medical report indicated that she was not even suitable for further rehabilitation services. The CAT scan showed that only analgesic medication and eventual surgery were possible treatments.

Georgia's friend Joan, who had persuaded her to go to a service, now insisted that she stand and claim the healing. Joan helped to lift Georgia from her seat. Slowly the two women moved down the aisle toward Grace, with Georgia literally dragging her right leg behind.

"Before Grace even touched me," Georgia recalled, "I fell back into an usher's arms. The next thing I remembered was trying to get up. I couldn't. My legs felt like Silly Putty, my back like a giant Slinky. There was no pain. But there was no strength either. This made me angry. There were people standing all around, and nobody was making an effort to help me get up. Next to me was a husky usher. He was just looking down with his hands stretched over me, praising Jesus. Grace was standing directly in front of me. She was doing the same thing, arms outstretched. Finally my friend Joan came over and began to lift me. But Grace stopped her. 'Jesus isn't done with her yet!' Grace said.

"With those words, I fell back onto the high school auditorium floor. A warm sensation flooded my entire body. There was a prickling along my spine. I have no idea how long I was out. Later, Joan told me that she began worrying that maybe I had gone into a coma or even died.

"When I came to, Grace told me to get up. I reached over toward the usher holding my cane. 'You don't need that anymore,' Grace said. She took the cane and winged it onto the stage, telling me that Jesus had made me whole again.

"Somehow, I got right up. Joan let out a gasp. It was the first time in nine years that she had seen me stand without any help. Then Grace asked how long it had been since I had climbed stairs. I told her it had been so long, I couldn't even remember. 'Well, praise God!' Grace said. She grabbed me by the hand and together we ran up the stage steps. The audience was out of their seats, cheering.

"Grace wanted to know, when was the last time I

danced? I told her that it had been nearly ten years. But before that time I had been an accomplished ballroom dancer. That was all Grace had to hear. 'Hallelujah!' Grace shouted. 'Let's dance for Jesus!' And we bounced around like two teenagers while the guitarist played 'Jesus Set Me Free.' "

Georgia waited a month before she went back to her doctor. When he saw her walk into his office without a cane or a limp, he was startled. He wanted to know what had happened. Before Georgia said anything, he examined her. He went down her back vertebra by vertebra and gave her a complete neurological examination that took forty-five minutes. It was the first time she had been able to do a heel-toe walk without falling over.

"There is absolutely nothing wrong with you," the doctor said, "except for a slight twisting of the spine. But that shouldn't cause you any problem."

At that point, Georgia told him about Grace and the miraculous healing she had received. She told him how, after that night, she had put her cane in the closet and never again touched it. She told him that she had a job and was now working full-time. She told him that she never touched the Percodan that she had been taking every three hours to control the pain. She told him that she had even enrolled in a ballroom dancing class and that since that night she had been walking on a cloud, with no pain or suffering.

As she talked about how Jesus had come into her life, a mask came over the doctor's face. "It's nothing but mass hypnosis," he said. He was somewhat hesitant.

Georgia didn't bother to argue. To her, it didn't matter if he believed in miracles or not. But she did mention that a year earlier she had gone to a noted specialist in hypnosis for pain reduction. At the end of the session (and a hundred dollars poorer), he told her that she was so resistant that no one could suggest anything to her; she was an impossible subject for hypnotic therapy.

These thoughts were going through Georgia's mind as she once again stood on the healing line. Grace moved down the line, touching everything from handkerchiefs to doll clothes, praying for those who couldn't be there.

"Praise God!" Grace said, standing before Georgia. "God did a good job with that back of yours." Grace rarely forgot a face or a healing.

Georgia realized that half the auditorium was waiting for healings. She couldn't take up too much of Grace's time with a lengthy explanation of what was wrong with her daughter. "My daughter has tumors," Georgia said. Tears filled her eyes.

Grace took hold of the photo. She pulled Georgia to her and said softly, "We're going to pray for those tumors to go."

As Grace prayed, Georgia felt that the only reason she was able to remain on her feet was that Grace was holding her. A surge of energy flooded her body: something was happening.

"Keep praising and thanking Jesus for your daughter's healing," Grace said. Then she moved to the next person in line.

Several days later, Georgia's daughter Laurie went to see her doctor. Because cancer ran in the family, the doctor was not treating her case lightly. Based on a pelvic sonogram test, exploratory surgery and a hysterectomy were distinct possibilities. On this day when Laurie came in, however, a second sonogram was performed, and the doctor was baffled by the results. He called in a consulting physician. Without saying anything to Laurie, the two of them went back to the results of the first pelvic sonogram, which had been taken only days earlier:

There is a rather large sonolucent structure measuring 6.4 cm. in greater diameter in the right side of the pelvis near the midline. Another, but much smaller one, measuring about 3.2 cm. in diameter, noted in the left side. These represent parametrial cysts. Structures of the pelvis, otherwise, are not unusual. No other space occupying lesion is noted.

Impression: Bilateral parametrial cysts.

"I don't understand this," the doctor told Laurie. "The cysts have completely disappeared."

For Laurie, there was nothing to understand. It was a miracle.

Shortly after my interview with Georgia Mathews, Bob Madison, the doctor whose ribs had been healed in spite of his skepticism, phoned me to call my attention to an article in *The New York Times* on healing that added credibility to what Grace was doing. It was the lead article in the science section. The headline read, LAYING ON OF HANDS GAINS NEW RESPECT.

In the article, researchers reported that they had detected distinct psychological effects from using a modified version of laying on of hands. It was called "therapeutic touch" for relief of pain. It included anxiety, increases in the amount of oxygen-carrying hemoglobin in the blood, and changes in brain waves indicative of relaxation.

The article went on to say that in a recent scientifically designed study at a major New York hospital, the results of this therapeutic touch could not be attributed to the placebo response. The patients were found to have improved even when they had no knowledge of what the technique was supposed to achieve. In this respect, the laying on of hands is quite different from psychic healing, because psychic healing depends on the faith of the patient. The therapeutic touch technique is often used in newborn nurseries to aid premature babies with respiratory problems.

It was indeed important evidence supporting Grace. When I phoned Bob Madison back, he agreed. "It's a very interesting piece. It'll certainly support Grace's case."

"Did it change your mind?"

"About what?"

"About it all just being the power of the mind."

There was a long noncommittal pause before he answered, "I'd like to see further studies done in the area."

"You still doubt that Grace is for real?"

"I never said that she wasn't for real. That night when Marian and I met her, I was more convinced than ever that she was legitimate. One hundred percent! People are definitely getting healed at her meetings."

"But are you still implying that it's only the believers?"

"The majority of them," he said matter-of-factly. "I told you before how I felt—faith will move mountains."

"But what about the skeptics who get healed too?"

"You mean like me?" he asked.

"Exactly. And the patients in the article who weren't even aware that they were receiving a healing. And yet they benefited."

"I was impressed by that," Bob admitted. "But I'd still like to see more documentation. If this can be scientifically repeated under controlled conditions, then you're talking about a major breakthrough in the medical world."

"You believe that there should be more research into the whole field of healing?" I asked.

"Absolutely," he said. "The bottom line is not who is affecting a cure. It doesn't matter if it's a doctor, a healer, or God. The important thing is that the patients are being benefited."

CHAPTER ELEVEN ❧❧

THROUGHOUT THE YEARS OF SEPARATION FROM her father, Grace continued to believe that someday they would be reunited. She didn't know how, when, or where—that she left up to God. But on July 30, 1983, she received a telephone call from her Aunt Agatha, her father's sister. Agatha was calling to say that she was bringing Grace's father up from Maryland to a service the following week. Grace made her repeat the message twice before the full impact struck. This had to be the working of God—there was no other explanation.

Grace didn't stop to ask how it had all come about. She was too overwhelmed. In one short week, she would see her father for the first time since the age of ten. Stunned, she hung up the phone to tell the rest of the family this latest—and most remarkable—of all miracles.

On the afternoon when Grace's father was due to arrive for the service, Grace and all her children were in the kitchen cooking for the family reunion that would take place the following day.

"Mom," Karen asked, "how old were you when Grandpa left?"

"Five," Grace said. "But I last saw him when I was ten."

"Do you remember anything about him?" Karen wanted to know.

"Just what I already told you, honey." Grace appeared to be jumpy.

"You mean, that he was a very unhappy man?" Karen said as she sampled some rice pudding. "And that he liked to gamble?"

"He had a rough life before he ever married your grandma. His own father beat him," Grace said, apologizing for his behavior.

Grace was careful this time, as she had always been in the past, to avoid burdening her children with the details of her own physical and mental abuse.

"But he loved you, Mom, didn't he?" Karen asked in a tone of voice that only wanted a positive answer.

"Oh yes," Grace said, "in his own way, he did."

Grace did not share what "his own way" was. There were only two occasions she could remember being held close to her father: the time he had carried her around the apartment to kill cockroaches with her bare hand, and the time he wrestled with her. He had wanted his oldest daughter to learn how to "beat up on her friends."

"How are you going to recognize Grandpa?" Christopher asked. He had come into the kitchen to see how his mother was doing with the cooking. "There will be thousands of people in the audience."

"Your father's saving the first row," Grace said. "Besides, Grandpa will be sitting with Auntie Anna and Cousin Eddie."

Suddenly the reality struck her with full force. In a

few short hours, she would be seeing her father for the first time in thirty years. Grace looked at the kitchen clock. It was almost four. They must be halfway here, she thought. She slipped two large trays of lasagna into the freezer and went into the bedroom to get ready for the seven-thirty service at the Westchester County Center in White Plains, where she had sung twenty years before.

At approximately four o'clock, George Tskanikas and his family crossed the Pennsylvania state line into New Jersey. They had been on the road since noon, and George was tired. He didn't like long car rides. More than that, he didn't like being pushed into this meeting with his daughter. A year earlier, Grace had phoned him; he had told her in no uncertain terms that he never wanted to hear from her again. George was a man of his word. Now, in front of his whole family, he would be breaking that word.

But George knew deep down that he couldn't wait to see his daughter. His second wife, Anne, and his son John had an inkling of this too. George's new sport jacket and shoes and his fresh haircut were an open confession. What his family didn't know was just how much he wanted to see her. When no one was around, George would play the album Grace had sent him. He would sit back, tap his foot to the beat, and study her photo on the cover. He could hardly believe how beautiful she was. To him, she was more beautiful than Sophia Loren. Her voice was even better than Peggy Lee's. This did not surprise George; from the time she was born, he knew that she was special: her soft, black curly hair, her large almond eyes, a smile that took up most of her heart-shaped face. She was singing before she could talk.

When George thought about Grace as a small child,

he also thought about her mother, Antoinette, and his own mother, Yaya. If it hadn't been for them, things might have turned out differently. They were always running off to church praying. As if that were going to make them rich or put food on the table or clothes on their backs. They were not in touch with reality. Never once did Antoinette give him credit for supporting the family. Instead, she made him feel as if he were a worthless bum. He had worked hard. Sometimes he would even stay at the pool hall for a week at a time. Hustling wasn't easy, even if you were the best in the field. One time he spent half his hustling money on a sirloin steak to feed his family. Antoinette wouldn't eat it because it was Good Friday. He should have realized right then and there that she was going to turn his kids into a bunch of fanatics.

At the George Washington Bridge tollbooth, John handed his father a copy of the ministry's magazine. A picture of Grace singing was on the cover. Behind her was a large white cross. It was dated August 1983.

"Dad," John said, "have a look at this month's magazine before we get there."

John was an accomplished musician. He had been invited to play at the upcoming service.

George was in no mood to look through the magazine. With one flick of his wrist, he flung it back at his son. "I don't want anything to do with her or that lousy religion stuff!"

"George! That's enough," Anne said in her pronounced Danish accent. When George recoiled, she softened. "You'll feel better once we stop and get something to eat."

Anne was easygoing, but this did not mean that she put up with her husband's tantrums. Several months after George and Anne had married, she laid down a house rule: If George ever so much as placed a finger on her or their children in anger, out he would go. Twenty-five years and three children later, George had not broken that rule.

Now George wished he had never agreed to go see Grace. It would be the first time he saw his grand-children. What would he say to them? What if they hated him? What about his son-in-law? Suddenly George wondered what Grace had told her husband about him. Well, whatever happened, he wasn't going to kowtow to anybody.

He had no regrets. If he had to do his life all over again, he wouldn't change a thing. He was a survivor. His own father had taught him how to survive each time he got a beating, each time he was denied food, each time he was thrown out of the house and warned that if he returned his head would be busted wide open. His father was another man of his word.

Shortly before seven, John dropped his mother and father off in front of the Westchester County Center while he went to park the car. A pale imitation of the Parthenon, the Westchester County Center accom-modates everything from sports events to concerts to dog shows. It was here, over twenty years before, that Grace had sung two solos on the same billing with Leslie Uggams and John Forsythe.

Arm in arm, George and Anne climbed the steps. Framing the entrance were two large posters of Grace. They read, COME AUGUST 6, EXPECTING YOUR MIRACLE FROM GOD. George could feel himself getting weak in the knees. "We're not going to have to sit here all night and put up with this garbage!" He spoke loud enough that the group in front turned around and glared.

People were filtering in from all directions. With a half-hour to go, the lower floor was already filled. Men in red jackets were directing people to the balcony. Grace had instructed Anne over the phone that when they arrived, they were to speak to one of the ushers. All the staff had been alerted that Grace's family would be arriving and that seats had been saved.

Neither Anne nor George expected to be seated in the very front row. Anne was delighted, but not George. "What are we doin' right on top of this shindig!" he said to the usher who seated them. Moments later, a different usher appeared. He handed George a small jewelry box and told him that it was a present from Grace. Inside was a gold pendant bearing the head of Jesus. Before George had a chance to resist, Anne had clasped it around his neck. This time he only quietly mumbled, "She knows I don't believe in this Jesus stuff. What's she doin' this for?" Then he swore.

"She did it because she loves you, George," Anne said. She grabbed hold of her husband's hand, partly as an affectionate gesture, partly to keep him from taking the pendant off, and partly to keep him from taking off himself. It had taken Anne thirty years to convince him to see Grace. Now that they had come this far, she intended to see that he went through with it.

A half-dozen of George's relatives had by now joined the family in the front row. George was ambivalent about the family reunion. He felt that his sitting there was an open admission that he had gone against his word. But on the other hand, George had to admit that he was impressed by the size of the crowd. "There must be five thousand people here," he whispered to Anne just before Grace came out onto the stage.

Backstage, the level of excitement was high. Ushers Joe and Al were on ladders hanging the newly designed dove of peace. Sharon and Karen were below helping Ron Mitchell to center four huge baskets of fresh flowers so that they were directly under the plywood dove. Larry James was doing a last-minute sound check and trying to get rid of some scratchy white noise in the speakers. Grace's husband had run out to the van for a roll of gaffer tape. Carol, the photographer, was adjusting the tripod of the video camera. It was almost seven-thirty.

While all this was going on, Grace was getting acquainted with her half-brother John. "I didn't even know I had a sister until a year ago," he told Grace as they embraced for the first time.

"I think we even look alike," Grace said. She backed up and looked at her brother. Her eyes clouded. "How's Dad?"

John, who was often told that he looked and played the guitar like Paul McCartney, smiled softly and said, "Dad's okay."

He didn't tell his newfound sister about the agony of the drive up from Maryland. Their father had groaned not only about being dragged up to see Grace but also about his youngest son taking part in the "religious shindig."

At fifteen minutes to eight, Grace said one final prayer and walked out onto the stage in between guitarists Larry James and John. She was singing "God of Miracles." This did not surprise Larry even though he happened to be strumming a different song; Grace often came out from the wings singing whatever she felt she had been led to sing, regardless of what Larry was playing. As far as Grace was concerned this song was apropos. To her, God was a "God of Miracles." Only a miracle could have brought her estranged father back after thirty years. During this first song, Grace avoided eye contact with the front row, where she knew her father was sitting. Then, as she was singing a second song, she spotted her two aunts, Agatha and Anna. Sandwiched between them was a man in a dark knit shirt. Without even focusing on this slender man whose gray hair was combed straight back, Grace knew that it was her father.

Two thoughts crossed her mind almost simultaneously: If their eyes met, would she have the emotional stamina to continue the service? Would her father think that she was pushing him into a confrontation with the Lord? George's last words to Grace over the phone a year earlier would not have made a good Bell Telephone commercial. He had told her in so many words that he never wanted to hear from her again, then he had slammed the receiver down.

Each time Grace looked in her father's direction, she meticulously skimmed her eyes over his head to the back rows. She had waited practically her entire life to see George. Now that he had come this far, she wasn't about to take any chance of losing him.

As Grace continued to sing, she was certain that she heard the inner voice of God, reminding her that He had promised time and again that one day her earthly father would return. With this divine promise clearly in Grace's mind, her confidence grew to such a degree that she felt as if she were about to explode with joy. Suddenly she moved to the foot of the stage, cued both guitarists to stop the music, and began to speak.

"Our God is here tonight to bless each and every one of you." Her arm waved over the audience to include everyone. "He's here to touch you. Save you. Heal you. And deliver you. You may not believe there is a God. You may be bitter against God. Maybe you've had a tough life," Grace said, her voice cracking. Larry picked up on that and began to strum in the background.

"Maybe you're sitting here tonight saying, 'If there's a God, He wouldn't have let me suffer so.' Maybe you're angry at God. But God didn't cause your unhappiness, your suffering. You caused it by not having Him in your world. But God's here not to punish you. He loves you. He wants to deliver you. When you come to know the Lord Jesus as your personal savior, the judgment is over. It is finished. You start a new life. Nothing ever again will be held against you. Everything you've ever done or said will be wiped clean."

Grace stopped for a moment. She swallowed hard and drew the back of her hand across her forehead. It was hot, and there was no air conditioning.

"Are you ready now to give yourself to God?" Grace asked. "To invite Him into your heart? Into your life? If you are, then please come forward." She backed up a few feet. Her arms were stretched out. "You'll have a new life in Jesus Christ."

With those words, Grace turned toward her father.

In the front row, George sat transfixed. He seemed uneasy. Nervously, he looked over one shoulder, then the other. People were getting up from their seats and coming down the aisle toward the stage. Grace's eyes, always piercing when she reached her most intense moments on stage, now focused directly on her father. He stirred in his seat. Then, with great effort, he began to rise. Slowly George pressed through the crowd toward the stage apron. Cousin Eddie and Aunt Agatha attempted to steady him in the crush. Singing "Please Search the Book Again," Grace began to sob. She knelt down and took hold of her father's hands. He looked up at her and said, "You're beautiful."

Still holding on to George's hands, Grace addressed the entire group in front of the stage. "Put one hand on your heart and one up to God and say, 'Father, I want your son, Jesus, to come into my heart and forgive me of all my sins. I'm sorry, Lord. I'm so sorry, Lord. Thank you, Father, that I am saved. That I'm ready to meet you at any time. Thank you, Jesus.' "

When the litany was finished, George repeated "Thank you, Jesus" three times in the silent auditorium.

"God just saved my father!" Grace shouted. Her voice was choked.

When the applause died down, Grace continued. "I've only seen my father once since the time I was ten. God promised me during the thirty years I've been praying that one day my father would return to Him and to me. You see, everyone, God answers your prayers."

"I love you, daughter," George said. Then he kissed her on the cheek and stroked her head.

"I love you too, Dad."

With that, two ushers boosted the sixty-six-year-old man onto the stage to join his daughter and son John. The three celebrated with a Greek folk dance. When the music stopped, George took his two children in his arms and cried.

Ten days later, Grace received a letter from her father. It was in his shaky handwriting.

11:30 Bless the Lord

Dear Daughter Grace:

I love you and always will no matter how much I hollered in the past. I didn't mean it. Something bad had a hold of me. My wife Anne wants me to be sure to tell you how much she enjoyed the visit. Everybody was so nice to us. I thought it was very nice of you being so nice to my wife. She's a good woman. It took her thirty years to get us together. Praise God, nothing will ever tear me away from you again. The trip home was very good. But I was tired. I slept from 10 PM till 10 the next morning.

My son-in-law is some kind of man. Larry worried so much about getting air into our tires, I thought he was going to take a heart attack of it. He must have stopped at 14 stations till he found the one with the pump working. Tell my grandsons and grand-daughters how much I love them and how I enjoyed that they took time to talk to their grandfather. Please tell me when their birthdays are so that I can send them something. I don't have much money but I want to get them a little something—just so they know how much I love them. I think you have made a very good job of raising my grandchildren. They are very delightful children. I enjoyed them more than anything in the world.

Your Aunt Penny had a hernia operation last week. But at 72 she is a good hearted old battle axe and tougher than me. The good Lord saw fit not to take her. Uncle Pete and Aunt Margaret came to visit yesterday. He tip-toed in at 369 pounds and left at 375. God bless his appetite. He sure can pack it away.

Well dear daughter I have to close now. I pray with all my heart and soul that you and your beautiful family have the best of all through Jesus Christ our Savior.

Your loving father,
George the Greek

P.S. I love you

203

Every week thereafter, George wrote, giving news of the relatives and life in Maryland. "Your half-brother John is getting ready to leave for Africa with the missionaries. . . . Aunt Agatha is recovering from bronchial pneumonia. . . . Baby Andrew is so cute I could just eat him up. . . . The doctor put Uncle Pete on a strict diet. I told Margaret she'd better get herself a padlock for the icebox. . . . We were snowbound for three days."

No letter was ever without a reference to Jesus or the Bible. After George returned home, he read the Bible, from Genesis to Revelation, memorizing certain scriptures as he went along. What George didn't understand, Grace explained to him when she phoned each week. Sometimes they would discuss one verse for over an hour.

This "new" George, however, aroused a certain amount of suspicion among his brothers and sisters. In a letter to Grace, one of George's sisters wrote, "I must admit that at first I didn't buy my brother's change. We were convinced that it was either a good act or he had gone soft in the head. Now, six months later, I'm forced to take that all back. I never knew that he had such a tender heart. George left Maryland like Al Capone and returned like the Pope. You now have me believing in miracles."

Grace wrote back, "Dear Auntie: God does not create junk. Every person alive has the potential to have what you called 'pope-like' qualities to shine through."

On August 4, 1984, Grace invited me to her house in Brookfield to meet her father. He had come up from Maryland with his wife and son to mark the one-year anniversary of his new life. I chatted with him across a picnic table spread with every Greek and Italian dish known to man.

Grace breezed back and forth from the screened porch to the kitchen, returning each time with a different platter. "What do you think of your daughter?" I asked.

"She's terrific," George said. "I love her." Then he turned to his wife sitting beside him and to John, across from him, and said, "I love all my family. I love everybody. And I wouldn't have said that a year ago. I would never let people inside my feelings."

"Why didn't you?" I asked, hoping that I wasn't overstepping my boundaries.

"I don't know why," he said. "Maybe because the Lord had to show me the way."

"Did you believe in Jesus before?" I asked, already knowing the answer.

"No. I believed only in the things I could accomplish with my own hands."

"But now you believe that there is a power greater than yourself?"

"Yes, ma'am," George said. He dabbed his mouth with a napkin. "God sets you on the straight and narrow. If you haven't got God with you, you got nothing. Nothing. I'm content with God."

"That first night you went to see Grace, did you think anything like that would happen?"

"No, ma'am. I had no idea."

"What did you feel when Grace touched your head?"

By now, I was confident that George wasn't going to get upset with my probing questions. When I had first walked in and Grace was introducing me to all the relatives as a writer, he had seemed to shy away.

"When Grace touched my head," George said, "I shook like a rattlesnake."

"How did you know that was God?"

"You know when something different happens in your body. Shock waves went through me."

"Shock waves?" I repeated.

"Yeah," George said. "It seemed like when she put her hand on my head, a bolt of lightning struck me down from the top of my head to my toes. It was the first time I knew there was a God. I had a peace and joy I never knew."

"Now you know there's a God?" I asked.

"As far as I'm concerned, there's a God. And if you haven't got God on your side, you're a lost person."

"The devil had a hold of you, Dad," John said. He reached across the table and squeezed his father's hand.

"I was the devil!" George said. "He had fun playing with me. Until you have Jesus, you don't believe in the devil. Jesus gets into you, He kicks the devil out."

"Hallelujah!" Grace said. She and the boys were clearing the dishes for the dessert.

"I'm not a total waste now," George said. He stacked a few plates and passed them to his grandson. "It's nice to know that you can get God into your life and your family."

"Dad," Grace asked, "if someone had said you'd get Jesus into your life, what would you have said?"

"No way, José!"

After dinner we sat on lawn chairs in the front yard. I studied George's face. I was convinced of his sincerity. My two-year-old son kept jumping on his lap for kisses. I thought of what Grace's mother Antoinette had once said: "Blind people and children are the best judges of character."

Of all the miracles I witnessed over the year I spent observing Grace, this quiet, personal miracle stood out above all the others. Her father's return had fulfilled an impossible dream. Sublime faith and devout patience had won out. Instead of the prodigal son, who left his family and was welcomed back, there was the prodigal father, received with the same effusive warmth and joy. The turbulence of the past had been replaced with a fresh inner peace that would carry Grace forward in her ministry with new and inspired vigor.

Afterword

By Grace DiBiccari

As I look back over the extraordinary events that have happened in my life, the miracles God has used me for, I've had to ask the question, Why me, Lord? Certainly it seems illogical that a housewife and mother would be used as a tool to bring forth healing powers.

I heard Billy Graham say long ago that whenever man gets to the point where he thinks he has God all figured out, it is then that God, in His divine wisdom, demonstrates His power and authority by doing something contrary to man's ways.

It was the Apostle James who asked the early church members, "Are there any sick among you?" If so, he instructed, "Let he who is sick call for the believers of the church; let them pray over him, anoint him with oil in the name of Jesus; and the prayer of faith will save the sick and the Lord shall raise him up."

It is this question, "Are there any sick among you?"

that is burning in my heart. I have seen lives ruined by sickness and failure turn around miraculously by anointed prayer.

As I search the Scriptures, I am reminded that the Lord not only taught the multitudes, but He healed them as well. It is this same Jesus who desires to reach out, through you and me, and offer a hand of compassion to a suffering world starving for His love.

For years, I had gone before the Lord and expressed my desire that He mend the relationship between my father and myself. To human eyes, it seemed impossible that such a reconciliation could take place. But one never learns faith and trust in easy circumstances. You cannot feel the depth of someone's sorrow until you've had a taste of it yourself. Even the difficult and abusive times have taught me to look up and see how I could learn to help someone else.

Then one day, as I stood on the stage singing a gospel song, I asked those who were ready to give their lives to Jesus to step forward. My father was one of the first to come. I embraced him, and we have shared a love for God and for each other ever since. Now I am blessed with the love and fellowship of two fathers, my heavenly one and my earthly one. That incident stands as a testimony to the power of prayer. God is a worker of the impossible.

I am often asked, "How does it feel to be used to heal the sick?" People wonder if there is ever a moment when I lose myself and think that I am privileged to possess the ability to work a miracle. I can only say that I never feel responsible for such an occurrence. In fact, my impressions are just the opposite. I am acutely aware that I am merely an instrument in God's hands, like a surgeon's scalpel or a maestro's baton.

Thousands of suffering individuals from all walks of

life fill the auditoriums and civic centers where we travel. I stand before them with faith in God, knowing that He cares for each one. He knows their needs, their illnesses, their desires. I minister to them, not by my own understanding, but by and through guidance—the word of knowledge that He gives to me.

I do not claim to have a new revelation, a new philosophy or doctrine. Nor do I believe that I am someone with unusual abilities. But I believe that all of heaven is waiting for the man or woman who will pay the price of full surrender and yield to His will, to the calling of God. It is then that God can take ordinary people and accomplish the impossible.

It is this message that I seek to bring forth: that a God of love is reaching out to us, but we must also reach out to Him. As we do, the greatness of His presence encourages us to spread love aand compassion to others.

I see greater works being done by the Lord's hand all the time. I believe that in the next several years, we will see miracles far beyond the scope of our imagination, miracles that will baffle the world.

Be confident that when you allow the Lord into your life, great things will prevail. For He brings help to the needy, hope to the hopeless, love to the unloved. God is our remedy. He can do the impossible for you.

ACKNOWLEDGMENTS

To THANK EVERYONE WHO HELPED WITH THIS book would be impossible. However, I would like to give special thanks to Larry James, the ministry's executive vice president. Without countless hours of his help, this book could not have been written. And to Carol Kaliff, the ministry's photographer, who went far above and beyond her call of duty in helping extensively with the voluminous research. In addition, I am most grateful to all of the volunteer staff members with Grace 'N Vessels of Christ Ministries for their generous help.